UTOPIAN Whispers

Moral, Religious and Spiritual Values in Schools

By the same author

Sense and Nonsense about God
Hellenistic Magic and the Synoptic Tradition
School Worship: an obituary
New Directions in Religious Education
Studies in Religion and Education
What Prevents Christian Adults from Learning?
The Act Unpacked: the Meaning of the Religious Education Clauses of the 1988
  Education Reform Act for Religious Education
God-talk with young children: Notes for parents and teachers
Mishmash: Religious Education in a multi-cultural Britain: a study in metaphor
Touching the Rock, an experience of blindness
On Sight and Insight: a journey into the world of blindness

UTOPIAN
Whispers

Moral, Religious and Spiritual Values in Schools

John M. Hull

RMEP

Religious and Moral Education Press

To
Edwin Cox
1916 – 1991

Religious and Moral Education Press
An imprint of Chansitor Publications Ltd,
a wholly owned subsidary of Hymns Ancient & Modern Ltd
St Mary's Works, St Mary's Plain
Norwich, Norfolk NR3 3BH

First published as *Utopian Whispers* 1998

ISBN 1 85175 157 2

The articles on which this book is based originally appeared as editorials in the *British Journal of Religious Education* and its predecessor, *Learning for Living*, over the period 1971 to 1995. The author and publisher would like to thank the Christian Education Movement for permission to reproduce these editorials here.

Designed and typeset by Topics – The Creative Partnership, Exeter
Printed in Great Britain by Brightsea Press, Exeter, for Chansitor Publications Ltd, Norwich

Contents

Chapter 3 Religious Education and Collective Worship in Policy and Practice

Chapter 4 The Agreed Syllabuses

Preface

In 1970, when John Bowden of the SCM Press invited me to become editor of *Learning for Living*, religious education was passing through an exciting period of development. The old assumptions about the relationships between Christian faith and religious education were giving way to a new, inclusive understanding of the subject. Religious education was moving out of its Sunday school background, and was becoming an educational subject, appropriate in the curriculum of the contemporary, pluralist school. During the twenty-five years of my editorship of the journal, which changed its title to become the *British Journal of Religious Education* in 1978, I was able to describe and monitor these changes. The result was more than 100,000 editorial words.

When I laid down the editorial pen in 1996, and passed the journal on to my successor Professor Robert Jackson of the University of Warwick, I gathered the editorials together and arranged them into two groups. The first group were mainly concerned with contemporary events, responses to recent reports and other publications, or descriptive introductions to the contents of special issues. However, there remained a large number of editorials which seemed to be of more enduring interest. I was encouraged in this belief by Terence Copley, who reviewed the editorials and published an appreciation of them in Volume 19, Number 1 (1996) of the journal. I was also encouraged by Mary Mears of RMEP, an encouragement which induced me to turn the editorials into the present volume.

Rather than arranging the editorials in chronological order, it seemed more coherent to group them into four main chapters. The first group deals with the emerging philosophy and theology of religious education. These form Chapter 1, 'Educational Religious Education', a title first used by Edwin Cox in an article he wrote in 1971 (reprinted in my 1982 collection *New Directions in Religious Education,* pp. 53–7).

The second group of editorials fall under the general heading 'Religious Education: Problems and Methods'. The last two chapters deal with the changing face of religious education over the past ten years, particularly in the light of the 1988 Education Reform Act and the controversies which continue to surround it. Thus chapter three is concerned with policies and practices in the light of the current legislation, and the final group of editorials deal with the implications of current policy and practice for agreed syllabuses and collective worship in schools.

The wording of the editorials has been changed in various respects. In the first place, the earlier ones were written in a style which was not sensitive to patriarchal language. In the early 1980s, when the *British Journal of Religious Education* adopted an inclusive style, it was amongst the first British journals to do so, but in the present collection this style has been adopted also for earlier material. Secondly, a number of references to immediate events or to the contents of a particular issue have been deleted, and an attempt has been made to improve the language where it seemed to require clarification. Finally, the tenses have been changed here and there, so as to enable the present-day reader to absorb the material without going into a time warp. It has not been possible to do this systematically, and here and there the original temporal viewpoint has been retained. It is thus possible for the reader to study the collection chronologically, using the dates in the heading of each item, or to approach the series thematically as suggested in the contents pages. Finally, introductions have been added to many but not all of the selections. Sometimes these introductions explain the original context of the argument. Sometimes they point to a later publication or influence which the article may have had. Sometimes a link is made with some present debate. On other occasions, an article seemed to require no such comment.

I would like to express my thanks to the Saint Peter's College, Saltley Trust who appointed me as their honorary research fellow in April of 1997. Without the time and resources which the Trust made available to me, the production of this book would not have been possible. I would also like to acknowledge the support which the Christian Education Movement has given to the journal over the years. It is an indication of the freedom and openness inherent within the Christian faith that CEM offered complete editorial freedom to the journal to develop an educational philosophy of religious education consistent with the Christian faith but not exclusive to it. I would also like to thank my colleague Julie Foster for her careful work in the preparation of the manuscript.

This book is dedicated to my predecessor in the University of Birmingham, Edwin Cox. When I came to Westhill College in Birmingham in 1966, Edwin Cox's seminal little book *Changing Aims in Religious Education* had just been published. For two years we worked together, and in 1968, when Edwin moved to the University of London Institute of Education, I was fortunate enough to be appointed as his successor. Edwin's continued insistence upon the need for religious education to make realistic contact with secularized young people representing many religious points of view and none continued to shape the subject in British schools until his death in 1991. This volume is dedicated to his memory and to the continuation of his work.

John M. Hull
OCTOBER 1997
University of Birmingham
School of Education

Introduction

The creation of a non-sectarian, publicly funded religious education for all children is one of the finest achievements of British education. This achievement, although distinctive, is not unique. With the exception of France and Albania, every major European country today has some kind of state provision for religious education. The new Norwegian world religions syllabus adopted in 1997 replaces the older Lutheran approach, and the German province of Brandenburg is experimenting with a new syllabus in world religions and ethics. In general it is becoming clear that the moral and spiritual values enshrined in its legacy of religions and philosophies is being recognized as offering an essential contribution to the European Community. Even in France, where religious education is generally confined to the Catholic school system, while the state schools are mainly secular, there is debate about the wisdom of this policy. It is being pointed out that if French young people had received a more informed understanding of Islam, then the problems of acceptance and adjustment being experienced by the Muslim communities in France might not be so severe.

One of the most significant features of the British achievement is its non-sectarian character. Even in Germany, where state-funded religious education still represents denominational interests, Roman Catholics and Protestants have not been able to agree on an integrated curriculum, while in Northern Ireland this has at last been achieved. In England and Wales the law requires that the teaching and practices of the principal religions including Christianity should be taught. The non-sectarian character of this enterprise means that although Christianity and other religions are to be taught, no attempt is to be made to advance the cause of one religion over another, or even to advance the common cause of all religions over or against the claims of a moral and spiritually sensitive humanism, except in so far as the religions are united in certain ethical and spiritual ideals.

The second noteworthy feature of the British experience is that religious education is rooted in local communities. The Agreed Syllabus Conference, and the Standing Advisory Council on Religious Education (SACRE) which every Local Education Authority in England and Wales is required to set up, constitute unique opportunities for discussion and collaboration about this vital aspect of the curriculum on the part of parents and members of the public acting through their elected representatives, members of the teaching profession and the religious bodies. This model of local community participation, unique to religious education, forms a striking contrast to the centrally dictated requirements which are typical of the other subjects of the basic curriculum.

Thirdly, religious education is taught by the regular teachers to the normal classes. Churches and other religious bodies have no formal influence on the selection and training of religious education teachers. In primary schools, the subject is taught by the ordinary classroom teachers, while in secondary schools, graduates in religious studies and theology are trained as specialists, just as are specialists in geography, mathematics and other subjects. In fact, religious education is a completely secularized branch of religious studies. This is one of its unique strengths. Moreover, it is taught to all children in the common classroom, regardless of any religious background which the children may or may not have. If Christianity were to be taught to Christian children by Christian teachers, and if Islam were to be taught by Muslim teachers to Muslim children, the public would soon start to ask why this should go on at the taxpayers' expense. The only justification for a publicly funded subject of this kind is that it is available to all children without distinctions of class, colour or creed. It is a contribution to the general educational and personal development of the pupils. After all, Christianity, like Islam and the other religions, has educational gifts to offer everyone, not only to the particular adherents of each faith.

Finally, British religious education is both critical and spiritual. It is critical in the sense that religious education seeks to dispel ignorance and superstition, exposing religious beliefs to the light of rational discussion. It is spiritual in the sense that it is not content with merely factual description but seeks to make a lively and intelligible contribution to the moral and spiritual development of every child. In both these respects, in being critical as well as spiritual, religious education is a characteristic product of the European Enlightenment. Every subject has a contribution to make to moral and spiritual development, but there can be little doubt that religious education is best equipped to lead this process.

Religious education can thus be regarded as the utopian whisper of the curriculum into the ear of Britain. The subject is utopian in the sense that it is a seedbed of hope. It represents the utopian hope that the religions of the world will abandon the relationships of futile competition which have been so typical of their history, and go forward together for the common moral and spiritual future of the species. It is a utopian hope that humanists and religious people will one day work together on this wider enterprise, as they already do in many SACREs. It is a utopian hope that religious education will do something to combat the Islamaphobia which is such a widespread feature of the image of Islam in the press and media in the West. Indeed, it is a utopian hope for the acceptance of children from all religious backgrounds and none, as all contributing to the British heritage of culture and values. Religious education does not distinguish our children from their children. Religious education believes that the potential for moral and spiritual growth can be awakened in every child.

However utopian its hopes might be, religious education remains but a whisper. This is partly because so many members of the opinion-forming aristocracy in Britain have not yet understood that religious education has emerged out of its sectarian past. They still regard it as an attempt to induce irrational belief in outmoded doctrines. This book is a utopian whisper in the ear of such cultured despisers of religious education.

Religious education remains a whisper in the sense that this is not an influential national institution, like the banks. When I read the unsolicited letters which come from banks in their thousands every week, inviting us to put our hopes in money and stirring up our greed and selfishness, and when I contrast this with the national statement on values published by the then School Curriculum and Assessment Authority (SCAA) in May 1997, the difference is striking. How can Britain assume its moral leadership amongst the nations if major institutions like banks which shape the lives and assumptions of millions of men, women and children make no attempt to incorporate the moral and spiritual values which lie at the heart of education?

Religious education is a utopian whisper into the ear of Britain. This book is presented in the utopian hope that it will make some small contribution to that whisper becoming a voice.

Chapter 1

Educational Religious Education

Christian Education as Christian Concern for Education

March 1971

I n 1970, when I was invited to take over the editorship of Learning for Living, *the predecessor of the* British Journal for Religious Education, *its sub-title was 'A journal of Christian education'. This title, however, had become ambiguous. Religious education could no longer be conceived simply as a process of Christian education.*

Although the title of Harold Loukes' 1965 book on classroom religious education was New Ground in Christian Education, *the following year saw the publication of Edwin Cox's* Changing Aims in Religious Education, *and the broader, more educational character of the subject was given greater form and substance by Ninian Smart in 1968 in his book* Secular Education and the Logic of Religion. *What was the relationship now between this new, broader kind of religious education and the process of Christian education as it had been previously understood? One of the major tasks of the journal in the years that followed was to develop this distinction. It was not until three years later that the sub-title of the journal was changed to 'A journal of religion in education'. With the passing of the 1988 Education Reform Act, there was a renewal of interest in the relationship between Christian education and religious education, so that this series of articles has an added interest today.*

A journal of Christian education?

What is meant by the sub-title of Learning for Living?

Our sub-title does not refer to the subject of the curriculum usually called religious education. It is becoming increasingly clear that in the county schools this subject can no longer be thought of as a process of nurture into the Christian faith nor can it proceed on exclusively Christian presuppositions nor may its content continue to be exclusively Christian.

Education as nurture into the Christian faith is the task of the Christian Church and it must act through its own agencies and institutions rather than through the state schools. The state's proper concern is with religious education of a wider kind. If the state accepts responsibility through its schools for the religious education of its children it must do so on behalf of all its children. No part of the curriculum should be devised so as to cater for one section of the community and to exclude others. The religious education offered by the state to children and young people today must be offered to the Christian family, the Muslim family, the humanist family, and to members of all other traditions without favour and without discrimination. It must be a religious education based not on an assumption that Christianity is true but on a belief in the importance of the study of the place of religions in the life of people.

Although, therefore, many of the articles in this journal deal with the teaching of religious education as a subject, this must be taken as an implication of our sub-title rather than as its direct meaning.

This journal is a journal of Christian concern for education. This includes particular interest in what is taught about religion in schools, but Christians are concerned for the whole of the educational process and for the conditions in which it takes place. A Christian concern for education includes a desire to enter into discussion with non-Christian educators, both those of other beliefs and those professing none. In such discussions Christians seek to listen and to learn as well as to speak and be heard.

Some years ago money was given by Christian Aid to rebuild a mosque which had been destroyed by an earthquake in the Middle East. This was a deeply Christian use for money. It has something to teach us about the role of a journal of Christian education today.

Learning for Living is a Christian journal in that it is produced by Christians and in that it seeks to express the nature and meaning of Christian faith by providing a forum for the unprejudiced discussion of educational issues, particularly those directly dealing with the teaching of religion in which all reasonable points of view will be represented. It welcomes contributions from people of good will and expertise, whatever their faith. It also hopes to help Christians engaged in education, in both Church and state, to explore the significance of the Christian faith for education. And here the first and most fundamental point to be learned is that Christians in education are not there to advance their own cause or to win selfish recognition for their own faith. They are there to serve.

Religious Education in Pluralistic Democracies

November 1972

The questions being asked about religious education throughout the Western World are remarkably similar. Discussion in the United States and in Canada, in parts of continental Europe and in all parts of the British Isles seems to be following a common pattern. Studies in New Zealand and Australia have indicated that the Antipodes is no exception. The crisis in religious education seems to be related in all these countries to the maturing of the concept of pluralism and to the role of education in pluralist democracies. If that is so, what is happening to religious education is part of a much wider development.

The questions being asked

In a series of seminars in schools, colleges and universities across New Zealand and Australia, from Dunedin to Perth, the questions asked were these: granted that religious education can no longer be seen as an attempt to foster faith, what ought its proper role to be? Are we reaching a position where we must conclude that just as the courts of law administer justice indifferently, so religious education must be indifferent to building the faith of the pupil? This would not mean that the courts do not care about justice, but that because they care, they administer it without favour or distinction. Similarly, ought not religious education, simply because it cares about education and about religion within the context of education, to teach it without favour or discrimination towards any particular religion? Ought we to conclude that the task of religious education is neither to foster faith in one religion nor to develop an attitude of general religiosity – whatever that may be?

Is religious education possible?

The process we are witnessing could be described as the secularization of religious education. It is being sharply distinguished from witness, confession and nurture and placed with increasing emphasis within the curriculum as a critical descriptive process intended to increase understanding. Can one foster understanding without fostering faith?

A theory of religious education?

A theory of religious education would need to spring from a theory of religion. But different understandings of religion yield different theories. The position is complicated by the fact that a theory of religious education needs to be firmly based on the psychology of religion. But is the psychology of religion sufficiently developed for this to be possible? It is increasingly clear that the dominance of Piaget's stages of development in religious education throughout the English-speaking world is a mixed blessing. Piaget's theory of the unfolding of intelligence is not adequate for religious growth. But from what source can Piaget be supplemented? We must look to psychoanalysis and to learning theory but the lack of experienced research workers in the area of applying such work to religious education must raise serious doubts about the degree to which solid progress can be achieved.

The church schools

As the gulf between religious nurture and religious education widens, the church-related schools find themselves in a quandary. One response is the tendency to form 'Christian' independent schools, where the curriculum will be 'based on the Bible' and all the members of staff will be Christian, but the attempt to create enclaves of nurture cannot succeed. Such places, because they tend to overlook educational norms, are likely to become known as schools the main purpose of which is not education.

The Church of England schools have indeed tended to fall between two stools. They have been too open in their intake and too exposed to pluralistic influences to successfully nurture. On the other hand, the provisions made for the teaching of religion in the classroom have often been so inadequate that there has been little opportunity for effective education either.

The nurture model

Provided that they do not neglect to provide a critical education concerning the religious area, it might be thought that the church schools should also nurture Christian faith. But although they might be entitled to offer nurture, one is bound to ask whether in fact this would be a wise policy for them to adopt. Mono-religious nurture was all very well in the Middle Ages when young adults might spend their whole lives as faithful members of the church and never meet a reasonable adult who would offer them any cause to doubt and never encounter a different lifestyle, but today this is impossible. Narrow Christian nurture may be able to produce faithful Christians but it cannot produce useful ones. For this reason the day of closed nurture is over and the churches in all their educational work, including that which takes place on Sundays, must accept the risks of a critical education.

Religion in state schools

Although there are variations from state to state, the general pattern in both Australia and New Zealand is that religious education is taught by the clergy assisted by teams of voluntary helpers. They visit the school once a week to give one lesson to each class. Sometimes the children are divided along denominational lines.

This system is breaking down. Some of the churches continue to look upon this system as representing an important sphere of church influence. In New Zealand the teachers' organizations are opposed to the introduction of religion within the ordinary curriculum because they fear that it would lead to 'religious tests' for teachers.

Hobson's choice?

In Australia and New Zealand the leaders of Christian and religious education face a difficult decision. They will be able to win for religion a place in the ordinary curriculum only if they can persuade the teachers that religious education would be free from evangelistic aims, but if that is made as clear as it needs to be, the churches will be deeply divided. It is possible that Christian educators would lose a good deal of their financial support and their personnel, so losing what little power base they have managed to retain. Meanwhile the acids of secularization eat deeper into the *status quo*.

Queensland

In Queensland the teachers' organizations have led the way in insisting that the government should do something about religious education. It is likely that RE will be introduced into the curriculum taught by the professional teachers and that the clergy's option of entering the schools will be suspended. This could be a most significant development and could point the way to a future for religious education in Australasia.

All in the same boat?

It is probable that as cultures continue to converge the future of religious education in the Western democracies will be one and indivisible. For this reason what takes place in Australia will continue to be watched closely from Britain, where, although within different structures, the same sort of problems confront religious education.

Religious Education and the Religions

May 1973

*A*lthough world religions had been taught, especially in sixth forms, for many years, and had been recommended in some of the progressive syllabuses of the middle and later 1960s, there was still a general tendency to assume that Christianity provided the norm and other religions were optional. However, the Shap Working Party on World Religions in Education had been founded in 1969 and the report of the Lancaster Project directed by Ninian Smart had been published in 1971. The conference which was to produce the 1975 Birmingham Agreed Syllabus was at work, and religious education was continuing its evolution towards pluralism.

In the last two or three years a major emphasis in religious education in Britain has been placed on teaching world religions. This is consistent with Christian faith and is required by the educational situation.

There are several aspects of the world religions trend which do not seem to have received enough attention. Perhaps the most interesting of these is the subtle change in the relationship between the religions and religious education. The religions have always been thought of as the *sponsors* of religious education. The religions have controlled the content of religious education. They have done this either through having their own schools or (as in the case of the Church of England and other Christian denominations) through their control of the agreed syllabuses granted by the 1944 Education Act. Religious education has been thought of as being for the benefit of the sponsoring religion. Even today, when an agreed syllabus is being drawn up in England, two of the four committees which constitute the legally required conference are composed of official representatives of religious bodies and only one is composed of the representatives of teachers.

This model is based on that which prevails in the church-controlled schools. In Catholic or Jewish schools, as in other religious schools, the religious body not only sponsors the school but also the religious instruction which is given. In the state system what we now have is actually only a shell of the old sponsoring relationship. Before 1944 state religious education was not even inspected by the state. Nevertheless the shell itself has only begun to crumble in the years since the world religions movement became dominant.

Not sponsors of study but objects of study

At least in the state system, the religions are no longer the sponsors of religious education but increasingly the objects of religious study. The religions constitute the subject matter of this part of the curriculum but the study is not intended to be either for the advantage or the disadvantage of the religions. As for which religions are to be studied and how this is to be undertaken, this is increasingly and properly becoming the preserve of the teacher. Religious people are the resources of the secular religious educator. The religions are the phenomena with which these particular teachers and pupils are concerned.

Will the religions accept this change?

No religion is finding this change of relationship easy to accept. When a religion has thought of this part of the educational world as being its legitimate sphere of influence, or has even built schools in order to maximize its influence in this area, it is not pleasant to discover that religious educators, the very ones who might be expected to be the front-line troops, are no longer willing to identify themselves first of all with the interests of the religious institution or to place as their number-one priority the spreading of religious faith. When for centuries you have had power to bind and loose, it is humiliating to be told that you are only a very interesting object of study.

The religions or religious denominations with their own systems of schools are to some extent insulated from this change because of the possibility of remaining a sponsor of religious education in their own religious schools. But the state sector in Britain is so large and influential that even the sheltered spots outside it cannot but feel the winds of change.

Probably the more recently established British religions such as Islam and Sikhism find the trend most difficult to understand. This is partly because of the beliefs about education which lie behind the movement for world religions in schools, beliefs which are on the whole European, not Asian. But many Christians and some Christian churches have similarly failed to realize how fundamental is the change taking place, and this in spite of the fact that many of the religious educators who have proposed the world religions are themselves Christians.

Christianity – a special relationship?

As the major sponsoring religion Christianity has always had a special relationship with state religious education. But Christianity is no longer the sponsor. No religious group is to have this role, nor are all the religions together to sponsor religion in schools. Nevertheless it must still be asked whether Christianity is to continue to have a 'favoured religion' status.

A number of factors might suggest that this should be the case. Christianity occupies a major segment of the religious phenomena which appear in the British Isles. Christianity provides the substratum of superstitions, beliefs and rituals which form any remaining links between semi-secularized people and the overt religions. A huge majority of the people who teach religion in school are Christians, often believing and practising ones.

These are important points. But it would be unjust and uneducational to claim that Christianity should therefore continue to be the faith into which pupils are nurtured, or the one which is presented to them seriously and in detail while the other religions are dealt with apologetically in the sixth form. On the other hand we can understand the nature of the 'special relationship' which must continue to exist between Christianity and religious education in Britain when we reflect that the acceptability of the world religions programme to the Christian conscience is more important to religious education than is the acceptability of the programme to (say) the Sikh conscience, since more Christians possess power in the teaching profession.

World religions and the Christian conscience

The Christian teachers are therefore in something of a dilemma. Not only are they asked to distinguish rather sharply between Christian education and religious education, but they are now asked to recognize that their faith is only one of the varied phenomena with which education is dealing and that in principle there is no more intimate connection between Christianity and religious education than there is between Islam and religious education.

Appreciation of these changes may involve for many Christian teachers of religion a rethinking of their whole vocation in education. Many teachers will go along with the world religion ideas, being pleased to attend conferences and delighted to be asked to take part in projects. But for some of them there will come a moment when they realize what is being asked of them. Then some will draw back.

The Christian teacher is probably not justified in drawing back. Of the various arks which offer themselves to the religious educator as shelters from the flood the world religions ark may be the most seaworthy. To convince Christian teachers that it is right for them to jump on with the clean and unclean beasts is a theological problem and then to persuade them to remain at the religious education helm is a major pastoral problem. The crisis of the conscience of the Christian religious educator in the British classroom is perhaps a crucial testing place in the dialogue between the world faiths today.

Religious Education as a Cluster of Subjects

November 1973

*R*eligious education has always been the focus for a number of interests, *and to those which were mentioned in this editorial, we would want to add the spiritual development of the pupil. Similar questions arise today about spiritual education as were being discussed in 1973 about moral education and so on. All subjects of the curriculum carry a responsibility for spiritual development, and we should not forget the fact that religious education, while it should occupy a central place in spiritual and moral development, also has its own specific subject matter: religion. It is doubtful if moral and spiritual education should be regarded as a subject in its own right, and the case for replacing any subject of the curriculum, including religious education, with an education in morals and values is not convincing. The most balanced moral and spiritual education takes place when students are helped to see that every field of human knowledge has its intrinsic moral and spiritual implications.*

Religious education in both the primary and the secondary school includes several areas of interest. Moral education is an important aspect but as well as helping young people to think about their personal values, religious education has been devoting a lot of time to *social concerns*. Some modern religious education is *social and political studies*, taught with an emphasis on values and in a general religious or at least broadly humanitarian framework. Some religious education is a sort of *sensitivity training* with an emphasis on the expansion of awareness and widening of the emotional repertoire. Religious education also includes a good deal of *ancient history*, mainly relating to Christian and Jewish origins, and increasingly it includes the study of such *non-religious lifestyles* as humanism and communism. Finally, and most important, religious education contains *religious studies* in the specific sense, i.e. the study of the religions of the world, their customs and rituals, their doctrines, their myths and their sacred writings.

A coherent cluster?

This group of subjects has been held together within religious education because of a philosophy which saw the various aspects as being part of the Christian enterprise in education. Teachers did not just teach the ethical problems associated with the use of money; they presented the teachings of Jesus about money. They did not only discuss the various sexual moralities which may be found in our society; they introduced their pupils to Christian sexual ethics. They did not only study problems of the Third World; they dealt with Christian Aid.

But what happens if religious education is no longer to be Christian education in this open and obvious sense? What happens to the coherence of religious education if the relationship between Christianity and religious education is no more intimate *in principle* than the relationship between Islam and religious education?

Moral education

The ethical teachings of the great religions are part of religious studies. Religious studies will naturally include Christian studies and this will be the place for Christian ethical teaching. But when it comes to the lessons dealing with 'human relationships' and 'problems of living' which are not presented as part of Christian studies, but are dealt with by the religious education teacher simply because this is part of the tradition of the subject and because such matters are important in their own right, then the teacher should not make such lessons a disguised form of Christian nurture. Teaching material now exists which presents moral education work-units in their own right and without reference to explicit Christian moral teaching. If in these lessons, the teacher uses materials supplied by Christian agencies and with specific Christian applications, he or she should make it clear to pupils that the material represents a Christian, or a humanist or whatever, point of view.

This being the case, there is really no longer any reason why religious education should continue to carry so much responsibility for moral education. Every subject has its moral implications, and it is encouraging to see how many books being produced for work in English and social studies are deeply aware of this.

Christian studies

Many of the older concerns of religious education must now be concentrated in Christian studies, where the final word indicates the general attitude which the teacher ought to adopt. The churches will become more important as providing the materials for Christian studies. But the fact that Christian studies will not be the whole of religious education suggests that a basic change in the agreement which takes place in the production of agreed syllabuses is called for. Previously, the parties agreed that what the syllabus taught was true. Now they can only agree that what the syllabus requires is worth teaching.

Christian concern for education

These developments make it a little easier to see something of the Christian role in education as a whole. Christians will be an obvious resource for the teacher of Christian studies. But there is no longer (if there ever was) any reason why Christians should think of religious education as being the most interesting and relevant part of the curriculum. This would be like thinking that the Christian ought to be primarily interested in the church. But the Holy Spirit is active beyond the church and the scope of the Christian concern in education is wider than religious education and indeed wider than the curriculum as a whole.

The centre of the RE cluster

To return to the question of religious education as a cluster of subjects, there is a danger that the subject area will fragment, or that teachers will become specialists in one aspect. One teacher will teach nothing but the Bible; another will teach nothing but personal relations; a third will concentrate on social and international problems. It is important that teachers of religious education should see clearly and insist to their colleagues, especially in integrated studies, that although they may have a wide range of human insights to contribute, their main offering is the religions of the world. The non-religious lifestyles have a place (which should be greater than it often is) but religion is the centre. Moral education may be the aspect or the alleged side effect most valued by the public; be that as it may, the central and proper content of religious education must remain not morals, but the study of religion.

Christianity and Religious Education

March 1974

N ow that the 1988 Education Reform Act has emphasized the need for religious education syllabuses to reflect the fact that 'the principal religious traditions in Great Britain are in the main Christian, whilst taking account of the teaching and practices of the other principal religions represented in Great Britain', the debate about the place of Christianity has received a fresh impetus. Indeed, the division between religious believers who are willing to share the curriculum with each other and those who find such an association uncomfortable has become sharper.

Until recently, the relationship between religious education and Christianity was not a burning issue. Teaching religion and teaching Christianity were the same. Religious education and Christian education were the same. What the church did and what the county school did were the same. Why then are we now asking about Christianity and religious education? The question is partly prompted by pluralism. Is the plurality of religions in British society to be recognized by religious education? It must be recognized if serious injustice is to be avoided in the schools. Are the religions to be treated in the same educational manner? They must be, for the same reason. The monopoly of Christianity is thus broken and from this break flow all the questions about the place of Christianity in religious education today.

Previous experience of pluralism

We have already had in England and Wales more than a century of experience of pluralism in religious education, but the pluralism has been Christian pluralism. It was the variety of Christian churches which created the limits of acceptable religious education, right from the start in 1870. It was the decision not to include specific denominational teachings which led to the emphasis upon the Bible. Everyone accepted the Bible. So the tradition in religious education, a tradition which still survives to some extent, that the main content would be the Bible, was the result of Christian pluralism. Today, however, the pluralism is wider. We now have not only a Christian pluralism but a pluralism of world religions. This is why the question, much debated as late as the 1960s, about the place of the Bible in religious education, has given way to the question about the place of Christianity in religious education. The question about the place of Islam in religious education must in principle be the same question. This does not necessarily mean that Christianity and Islam can be taught in the same way or for the same amount of time. But it does mean that no religion can claim to control the general intentions of the subject or provide an exclusive rationale for it.

Is Christianity just another religion?

This is the question most often asked about the implications of teaching Christianity alongside other religions. Christianity is obviously a religion, and like several religions, it contains principles by which to judge both other religions and itself. The very respects in which Christianity is unique can only be established after a comparison with similar aspects of other faiths. We must therefore speak of Christianity (like other faiths) as having points of both difference and similarity and not seek for a monolithic uniqueness which would forbid all comparison.

The sting in the question comes with the word 'just' – 'just another religion?' The word 'just' suggests a note of disdain towards other religions. This disdain is often sensed by non-Christians and is often the feature of Christianity most repellent to them. Before we can answer the question, we must hear it through the ears of people of other religions.

Christian humility – and pride

The transformation of Christian religious education into religious education containing amongst other subjects Christian studies depends upon the emergence of a kind of humility which will no longer speak of being 'just another religion'. Christianity is at least another religion and need feel no shame at being associated in the curriculum with the other great faiths.

It follows from the last point that Christians ought to express their pride in their faith not by trying to control for narrow religious reasons a certain subject of the curriculum, but by the quality of their work as educators and by their concern for a just society.

Christian Faith and the Norms of Education

Winter 1975

Modernity represents the rule of the Enlightenment, with its belief in universal rationality. Post-modernity refers to the change which is said to have overtaken modernity, a change which leads to the decay of grand theories and world histories. Post-modernity is less interested in overarching rational principles and more aware of the particularities of local cultures.

The change in mood between 1975 and 1998 is typical of the shift from modernity to post-modernity. Then, the debate was more about general rationality; today, a greater recognition of cultural diversity and a greater awareness of the dangers of mistaking European ideas for universal truth has encouraged us to accept more readily the needs and rights of distinctive ethnic and religious communities to seek their own distinctive styles of education. However, this does not mean that modernity is swallowed up in post-modernity. Religious and community traditions are important in education, but they are not absolute. Education is indeed relative to community needs, but community needs must be interpreted in the light of wider social needs, and ultimately in the light of what being human itself may mean. On the one hand, there are as many religious educations as there are religions. On the other hand, a critical, enquiring religious education has a special responsibility, both to the individual religions which support it and to society as a whole, which needs it.

Paul Hirst, formerly Professor of Education in the University of Cambridge, presented an important article called 'Christian education: a contradiction in terms' (*Learning for Living* 11, 1972, pp. 6–11). Professor Hirst claims that '... there has now emerged in our society a concept of education which makes the whole idea of Christian education a kind of nonsense'. The substance of this so far is found as the fifth chapter of Paul Hirst's book *Moral Education in a Secular Society* (University of London Press, 1974). There may be distinctively Christian, humanist or Buddhist concepts of 'primitive education'. This is the view which a 'primitive tribe' might have of education as the uncritical passing on of customs and beliefs, and according to this view, 'Christians seek that the next generation shall think likewise'. But when we come to education marked by concern for objectivity, for knowledge, for truth and for reason, then '... there can be no such thing as Christian education'.

Nothing to contribute

These claims are supported by a discussion of the nature of the secular society, which, Professor Hirst suggests, is characterized by '... a decay in the use of religious concepts and beliefs' leading to the situation where religious beliefs

'... come to be seen as of no consequence, having nothing to contribute in our efforts to understand ourselves and our world and to determine how we are to live'.

Professor Hirst thinks that the position he outlines between the Christian faith, society and education is one which many Christians might be able to accept. Considerable attention is given to the problems created for Christian life and faith by the argument of the book, and when the critical, sophisticated view of education is discussed, Hirst thinks that '... it is precisely the concept of education an intelligent Christian must accept'.

Hirst claims that Christian belief has nothing to contribute to the theory of education. When he says that intelligent Christians ought to accept the critical, rational view of education, he means that Christians should accept it in so far as they are intelligent, and not in so far as they are Christians as such. For if the latter were the case, these intelligent Christians would be accepting this modern view of education because it flowed from the nature and structure of Christian faith itself. We would then have a constructive relationship between Christian theology and this sort of education and thus a Christian philosophy of education, but this is the very thing which Hirst denies. It is, he thinks, impossible in principle as well as unobtainable in practice.

So we have apparently reached a breaking point in the relations between Christianity and education. It is no longer possible, if Hirst is right, to think one's way from the Christian faith to education. This is not a question of the survival of religious education as a subject of the curriculum. Hirst has been understood by some as wishing to abandon religious education in school. It is distressing to see how frequently anyone who makes unusual suggestions about the role and nature of this part of the curriculum will be interpreted as wanting to abolish it. This, however, is far from Hirst's mind. Anyone who studies his writings from about 1965 will find that he has never wavered in his support for a thoughtful, open-ended, descriptive study of religions in school. What he denies in *Moral Education in a Secular Society* is something much more profound and serious than the fate of one subject. He denies that in principle there can be constructive relationships between religious beliefs and open, critical education as a whole.

Quite a serious matter

We are accustomed to say that religious education, as a school subject, must be justified on purely educational grounds rather than on theological grounds. Theological grounds alone are insufficient. But are they also improper in principle? Not only can we not rely upon theological grounds but, if Hirst is correct, they cannot be brought forward at all. Although religious education must be justified on educational grounds, how are we to justify the educational grounds themselves? Granted that theological considerations cannot determine what is good or bad in education, cannot such grounds even illuminate? Can there be no proper religious scrutiny of education at all? If this is indeed the case, it is hard to see how any thoughtful Christian (or Muslim or Jew), desiring to live a life in unity with his or her faith, can do so within education. Hirst is aware of this, which is why he tries so seriously to commend his position to the Christian believer. But if he were to succeed in his claim that there can be no Christian education, and to fail in his effort to commend this to Christians, it would be a matter of some importance for the future of the whole religious enterprise in education.

But does he succeed?

It is difficult to see that Hirst has succeeded in either part of his project. He has, in our view, failed to commend his position to Christians, but since he has also failed to show that there can be no useful relation between Christian belief and education, his failure to commend that view to Christians does not matter.

Hirst claims that secularization means that a subject is autonomous and free from religious control. He does not point out that there can be many forms of relation between religion and education which may still be significant although they fall short of control. In his discussion of the relation between Christian faith and the secular moral life, Hirst shows that the Bible, interpreted thoughtfully, supports just this kind of approach to morals, and that therefore we can speak of a Christian view of the moral life which fully respects the autonomy and secularity of morals. Why then cannot we speak of a Christian view of education which respects the autonomy and secularity of education? Hirst speaks with approval of those secular theologians who have supported, on Christian grounds, the secular city. Why should there not be Christians who, on exactly the same grounds, will support secular education within the secular city? Then we would have a Christian view of education just as we have a Christian view of morals, namely, one which sees education as free, open and enquiring. Christian faith would not, of course be the only ground from which such a view of education could be derived. It would not control or determine such education. That does not mean that it must be denied any contribution at all. Christians do not claim that only Christians can become educators. They wish only to find it possible for some educators to remain Christians.

Hirst's failure to make these distinctions seems to spring from a failure to appreciate that the degree to which a given theology can generate an understanding of education may vary widely. Not all theologies can escape the danger of which he is so well aware – the danger that the religion consumes the education, turning it into something more primitive, which becomes merely the passing on of uncritically held assumptions. However, because not all theologies escape the danger, we must not conclude (as he does) that all theologies fall into it.

How to do it

Hirst thinks that there are various ways in which a Christian philosophy of education might be attempted, but that they lead to nothing. His ideas about theological method are not very subtle. One might, he suggests, begin with what is said in the Bible about education and try to apply this to teaching today, but problems such as the cultural remoteness of the Bible and the controversies surrounding its interpretation make this so difficult that '... a distinctive Biblical or Christian view of education simply is not discoverable'. This conclusion is bound to follow when sophisticated educational thinking is contrasted with simple theological thinking. To a reader more familiar with discussions of theological method today, and with the complex and careful work of theologians such as Bernard Lonergan, Ray Hart, Walter Ong and Gregory Baum (to name but a few), Hirst's conclusion about the futility of theological method might seem a little premature.

Christian Nurture and Religious Education

Summer 1977

In seeking to participate in the education of the wider society through participation in general religious education, religions themselves undergo a process of education. This leads to a distinction between the natural interest which each religious tradition has in perpetuating itself – what we might call the interest in the nurture of faith – and its interest in the promotion of the moral and spiritual development of society as a whole, through contributing to the general search for values by which to live. A religious tradition unable to make this distinction will seek to impose its own faith and nurture upon the schools, which will inevitably lead to the destruction of the idea of a general religious education for all children. In the extract which follows, the implications of this dual role are worked out in the case of the Christian faith. The discussion to date has been widened by the participation in increasingly equal terms of other religions, and made lively by the tendency on the part of some religious communities to fall back into the assumptions of uncritical faith nurture.

'Are you a Christian?'

It is not uncommon at meetings connected with religious education to hear it suggested that speakers advocating contemporary approaches in the subject are probably not Christians. The people who ask this kind of question at conferences and lectures are seldom interested in the factual question concerning the religious affiliation of their speaker – they are not asking if he might be a humanist or a Hindu. The implication is that there is something about contemporary religious education which Christians as a group would probably not support. Such questions are usually asked in a rather hostile manner: the speaker is sometimes almost dared to admit that he/she is not a Christian, and to come clean, and confess, so that everyone can see the sort of position from which these outlandish ideas are springing.

What are the aspects of modern religious education most often thought to be incompatible with Christian faith? The critical questioners we are describing usually suppose that a Christian could not really believe in teaching world religions, and must be utterly opposed to the teaching of the secular ways of life. Christians are expected to support compulsory Christian school worship and, above all, Christians are expected to call their pupils to Christian faith, seek to extend the personal allegiance to Christianity throughout the school, and nurture Christianity rather than to religiously educate.

Christians and religious education

In 1975 the Christian Education Movement General Council recommended for discussion a statement, prepared by a specially appointed committee, called

'Christians and Religious Education'. This brief but important declaration has become fairly well known within CEM itself, but has not been much talked of elsewhere. The statement is as follows:

> Religious education, being part of education as a whole, enables pupils to explore in the field of religion. As a component of general education, it rests upon and requires values such as rationality, sensitivity and integrity, but it is open in that it does not assume particular religious belief or disbelief at the beginning or seek it as the end of the enquiry.
>
> An understanding of the relationship between commitment and openness is vital for the Christians engaged in religious education. Christian commitment is to the living God who continues to rule history, and who reveals through Jesus Christ, the incarnate and risen Lord, and still leads God's people by the Holy Spirit, the Spirit of Truth. The attitude of openness, trust and hope, symbolized by the Biblical image of pilgrimage, is characteristically but not exclusively Christian. Therefore Christian commitment to God leads us not only to enquiry in theology but also to a view of religious education as an open, critical process.
>
> It is proper, therefore, for the Christian Education Movement to continue to promote religious education including an open, critical exploration of, for example, world religions, religion and life in both history and contemporary society, and to do so not in spite of its Christian position but because of it. Far from acknowledging any contradiction between the Christian's confession and his/her professional responsibility as a teacher of religious education, we believe that Christian faith informs and illuminates this professional task.
>
> The faith and practice of Christians have become one object of study among others within religious education. There is thus a dual relationship between the Christian and education. As a Christian he/she is part of the religious phenomena to be studied, and equally as a Christian, he/she is engaged in a critical scrutiny of education, including religious education. This means that Christians and the churches to which they belong ought to encourage both aspects of this relationship. The Christian Education Movement should continue to present itself as a committed Christian organization making a valid educational contribution. It should provide for these distinctions by working for the development of religious education, for a Christian critique of education and for the Christian nurture of teachers of young people in voluntary

associations and activities. Its nurture of Christians in commitment and openness, and its promotion of critical religious education flow from one and the same Christian faith.

The first paragraph points out that religious education is both committed and open. It is not neutral, since it rests upon values, but since its main emphasis is upon exploration of religion, it does not set out to deepen Christian faith, or to foster any other religious or non-religious belief. There is a general commitment to the exploration, but specific commitment to a given religion is neither assumed nor sought.

The second paragraph takes up this central theme of commitment and openness. This relationship is expressed in traditional Trinitarian theology, such that both commitment and openness flow from faith in God as Father, Son and Spirit. This is brought out partly by describing the activities of God in the present tense ('continues to rule') and partly by stressing the life and movement within the Christian idea of the Trinity. So God is 'living', ruling 'history', is revealed, Jesus is 'risen', the Spirit will lead us into truth. Trinitarian faith is dynamic, not static; it is itself a questioning, truth-seeking activity. This is supported by a reference to the idea of the moving, travelling people of God in biblical thought. The final sentence of this paragraph claims that the self-critical theological enterprise of the Church (surely one of the glories of Christianity) and the idea of a critical, open education flow from the same complex of Christian ideas, but the statement is careful not to claim a monopoly of critical openness – such ideas are 'characteristically but not exclusively Christian'. The CEM certainly does not claim that none but Christians can have such ideals of religious education. All it claims is that Christians are decisively impelled towards such a view of education.

The third paragraph draws conclusions for religious education, including the world religions emphasis and the current stress on teaching about religions in their contemporary setting. It has been the practice in recent years to distinguish between the 'professionals' in religious education (those who are in the first place speaking as trained and practising teachers) and the 'confessionalists' (those whose first interest is in representing or promoting a particular religion or denomination). The CEM statement regards that distinction as being invalid, at least in the case of Christianity and probably other religions as well. Christians of the sort described here are professional in their training, practice and standards precisely because they are confessional. We believe in teaching world religions not in spite of our Christian faith but because of it.

Christian nurture

The final paragraph distinguishes Christianity as being scrutinized in education and Christianity as scrutinizing education. Christianity is evaluated in religious education. Christianity also has a duty to evaluate religious education. Since Christianity is also (by its nature) committed to self-evaluation, there is no tension between these two activities, and the Christian task is to encourage both. In the same way, the Christian is involved in Christian nurture (in the church or 'para-church') as well as religious education. Again, there is no tension between these activities, although there is a vital distinction which must always be carefully observed.

In this statement we have a succinct reply to the good people who think that a Christian could never seek anything but the cause of his/her own party, and could never wish that one should become anything other than a replica of himself/herself. Here we have a reply to those who think that a Christian could keep children unaware of diversity, ignorant or reasoned opposition, and uncritical of their own traditions.

Religious Education and Modernity

Summer 1987

One of the special features of religious education in Britain is that pupils from several religious backgrounds and from none are all educated together in the one classroom, from a single syllabus, taught by one teacher. This situation raises questions about the identity of both individual pupils and of the religious traditions themselves. These are the special features of modern religious education which are so typical of modernity, and which make it possible to describe religious education as both a product of and a carrier of modernity.

The word 'modernity' is used in the social sciences to summarize the features of that form of contemporary society which, originating in Europe, has now spread throughout the world. It is characterized by industrialization, urbanization, bureaucratization of government, and the formation of huge, impersonal structures such as industrial corporations, organized professional life, departments of government and so on. One of the features of modernity is secularization, although it is increasingly recognized today that this is but one of its aspects, and not necessarily the most important for religion.

Ideologies

Modernity has been called the age of ideologies. Pre-modern societies tended to be dominated by a single, prevailing world-view, for example, Christianity in medieval Europe, although there have certainly been periods of past culture characterized by pluralism of one kind or another, such as the Hellenistic culture of the third and fourth centuries CE. Pluralism is, however, an intrinsic feature of modernity, and studies of ideology have become increasingly important in recent decades in an attempt to understand the social and individual consequences of belonging to a minority which has a particular view of the world.

If we remember that the first European system of state-controlled education emerged in Prussia in 1717, we can see that education as we know it is also a characteristic of modernity. Education itself is one of the vast, anonymous structures of modern Western society, and it is characterized by industrialization (teachers on strike think of themselves as taking industrial action), bureaucratization (the increasing tendency to formalize professional norms on contracts and legislation) and, above all, pluralization. One way of looking at the work of the religious education teacher today is to consider him or her as a carrier of modernity, the specialist in that part of the curriculum which deals specifically with the pluralization of contemporary consciousness and the conflict between contemporary world-views. This is not to say, of course, that the teacher of science and of computer studies does not occupy an equally significant, although different, place in the school as an expression of modernity, and we should remember that the whole concept of the curriculum itself is related to the social status of knowledge and so on.

Ideological enclosure

One response of a social group with a particular world-view, when it is placed alongside and in competition with another world-view, is to try to contain the emotional and intellectual life of the members of its own group, to isolate them from alternative points of view. One of the important processes of such containment is education, and we notice within all of the self-consciously 'different' groups around us today, whether obviously religious such as the Muslim or Christian communities or more psychological such as the various human-potential groups, a powerful emphasis upon educational techniques, both for adults and for their children.

One of the reasons why modern religious education is so precarious and so exciting is because, as the process is understood in British schools, it deliberately sets out to resist ideological enclosure. There is an 'escape clause' still on the statute books for those parents who find it quite unacceptable that their children should be taught faiths other than their own, but for the vast majority of British young people, religious education today offers the main way whereby the plurality of the modern world is recognized, and dialogue between alternative world-views is encouraged.

This does not mean that exposure to modern religious education should weaken the commitment of children to their own family religious traditions, if any. It is not only appropriate but inevitable that human value and meaning should be organised into coherent world-views, and that these should vary one from another. Religious education is just as much concerned that pupils should reside within their ideologies in an intelligent way as it is that they should not be entirely enclosed by their ideology. It is the totalitarian tendency rather than the ideology as such which religious education exposes.

Nurturing ideological commitment?

This means that although modern religious education does not seek to nurture faith in a particular commitment, it may nurture intelligence and criticism within the commitment. There is a nurture of faith which is appropriate for religious education when one thinks of it as a carrier of modernity, in the context of competition between ideologies.

27

Ideology and identity: religion and personal development

The psychologist Erik H. Erikson once remarked that religions offer ideologies to youth in search of identities. Ideologies structure our language and our thought. They order our patterns of self-understanding and community life. Ideologies possess a person-making power. They generate identities. This is why there is such a powerful connection between religious education and personal development.

Emerging from identity

Your identity is most secure when you are not even aware of it. You only ask the question 'Who am I?' if your identity is already under threat. The familiar experience of culture shock illustrates this. It is when our way of life is placed under question, when we go abroad for a while, that we become self-consciously British, or French, or whatever.

This is true not only of individual identities but also of entire social groups and their ideologies. When an ideology becomes sharply aware of itself, it is already under question. It was only after the break with the Eastern Church in 1054 CE that the Western Church began to think of itself as Catholic in a very special sense. It was only after the Protestant revolt and the work of the Counter-Reformation that the Western Catholic Church became even more self-consciously Roman Catholic, and in the acute modernity of North America, Catholicism has become a denomination.

The American psychologist Robert Kegan in his 1981 book *The Evolving Self* has described what he calls 'the holding environment' of the self. This is the social context which confers identity, and which is normally taken for granted. For the young child, it is the family. For the mature child, it is the peer group. For the adolescent, it is the group of intimate friends. Only when a person begins to emerge from it does that holding environment itself become an object of reflection and self-consciousness. The adolescent, emerging from family, becomes critical of family. The adult, emerging from national enclosure, becomes critical of nationality. That emergence creates an emergency, since the self no longer has a secure, holding environment. One way of making meaning of the self in the world is being exchanged for another. This notion is experienced as emotion.

To become aware of one's own ideological position is to begin the process of emerging from it. One of the effects of modernity is to create emergences of this kind, and both individuals and groups experience the consequences. Does this mean that immediately one becomes aware of the fact that one is a Hindu or a Christian, one has emerged from that world, to some extent? Has one become, in some way a *worse* believer? Just as children's experience of junior school is bound to lead them away from total enclosure within the family, is religious education bound to lead pupils away from a simple faith? Is a simple faith a better faith? Education, whether religious or secular, must always encourage personal development, including reorganization of self at more complex and more effective levels.

Mono-religious schools

Since religious education must lead children and young people, sooner or later, to break the bounds of their earlier religious identities, it is understandable that there should be a demand for separate school systems drawn up along ideological lines, i.e. dominated by one religion. There would thus be a rejection of the relativizing tendency of an all-embracing school system. There would be a fear, perhaps an understandable one, that the ideologies would be trivialized by their inclusion within a world religions syllabus.

When we look at the history of religions, however, we see a series of emergences from earlier, simpler world-views. The American sociologist Robert Bellah has offered a history of stages of religious culture, from primitive religion through classical to the religion of modernity. There may well be an affinity between the cultural development of religion as a whole and the religious development of the individual. Identities and ideologies may pass through similar stages of maturity. We may thus think of each ideology as encouraging its adherents to pass through a series of emergences, in which they will learn individually what the ideology itself has learned. They will mature as the ideology has matured. On the other hand, we may ask whether ideologies resist passing from one stage to the next, just as we may ask whether and why an individual may resist a new stage. What helps an ideology grow? What helps an individual grow?

The troubling of identity

We can see, then, that it is not the task of religious education to foster identity. It is the religion, the ideology, that does this. The task of religious education is to trouble that secure identity, to initiate an emergency from which a complex but more adequate identity may arise. Religious education, in other words, offers personal development through ideological criticism.

Questions for curriculum development

From this discussion we can draw a number of questions which could be put to any religious education curriculum. Does the religious education curriculum disturb and unsettle the pupil's sense of identity? Does the curriculum offer help to pupils by drawing upon the internal, critical and developmental power of the religion being studied? If, for example, religion is taught as having only the characteristics of primitive or classical religion, how will that help pupils to reach an integrated outlook consistent with modernity? Does the experience of pupils in religious education classes help them to negotiate with the characteristics of modernity and with religious modernity? Does the religious education department offer a 'pilgrimage' curriculum in which spiritual development is actively encouraged, or is it merely a matter of transmitting certain facts within a framework which takes modernity for granted? What attitude does the curriculum take towards ideological enclosure? Is this holding environment taken for granted? Is it, on the other hand, taken for granted that there is no holding environment, that pupils come without commitments, without values? Does the religious education curriculum challenge the pupil by offering diverse and even conflicting spiritualities? By what means are pupils enabled to appreciate those spiritualities?

Religious education is not only a carrier of modernity; it must enable pupils to confront modernity critically. In that way, what happens in religious education classrooms will make a small contribution not only to understanding modernity but to going beyond it.

Commitment and the Teaching of Religion

Autumn 1985

As Christian nurture developed into religious education the character of the vocation to become a religious education teacher also changed. Christian nurture proceeds from faith to faith, but religious education is taught by any well-trained teachers of goodwill regardless of their personal faith and is offered to children from all religious traditions and none. What kind of commitment does the teaching of religious education demand?

What is the popular attitude towards commitment today? Commitment is seen as a prison. Commitment narrows one's loyalties, and restricts one's freedom. Commitment closes the future. Commitment is boring, because there is no longer any suspense, innovation or questioning. To commit other people is to invade their privacy and to insult their right of self-determination. To commit oneself beyond today is to deny the uniqueness of the historical moment in which one will be found tomorrow. The uncommitted person is more adaptable, more available, more flexible. When one says of somebody that he or she is committed, one says it with the same tone of voice that one uses when saying that he means well, or that she is very sincere. Commitment, sincerity and meaning well are the virtues of the middle-class, middle-aged professional do-gooder.

This is the image of commitment in the late twentieth century. This is what commitment looks like to many people in Britain. This is how people feel about it. The Enlightenment of the eighteenth century reacted against the commitment which had led to the religious wars of the seventeenth century, and the enlightened popular rationality of the late twentieth century is in reaction against the ideological commitment which marked the middle years of the twentieth century and which was expressed in the Second World War.

Religious education and the heritage of commitment

If we read the Christian educators of the period 1920 to 1960 we are amazed at their commitment. They were committed to the faith and to freedom, democracy and education. They were against fascism, communism, humanism, technology, industrialization and modernity. In their steadfast Christian commitment they had a horror of diversity, suppressing and ignoring even the limited variety of beliefs which existed in the Britain of their day, and trying, because of their commitment, to create a religious education which would be as single-minded and as pure-hearted as the naive and romantic Christian faith from which it sprang.

Religious education and the reaction against commitment

It is not surprising that the religious education teachers of recent years have rebelled against this image of their profession. In this, they have been in tune with the ethos of the seventies and the eighties. As the philosophers of education have increasingly emphasized autonomy as the goal of education, and as the increasing pluralization of British society has brought home to everyone the variety of commitment from which one can choose, selection and enquiry rather than obedience and commitment have become the very atmosphere we breathe. The world religions syllabuses expressed this ethos and emphasized it. One was no longer teaching for commitment but for understanding, and one's teaching no longer proceeded from commitment but from professional training and skills. So what Peter Berger in his 1980 book called *The Heretical Imperative* of faith became the educational objective of the religious education teacher.

Commitment versus values

The attitude towards commitment expressed in our opening paragraph conceals a dilemma to which many people today, especially the young, are sensitive. If commitment is a prison, apathy is a betrayal. Commitment is out, but values are in. Lifestyle, ecology, the questions of nuclear warfare, political responsibility and Third World development demand that certain values should be maintained. This, then, is the dilemma of the modern person set 'free' from the authoritarian religious traditions and the kind of commitment they represented only to find that if commitment debases humanity, humanity demands values. But having to have values implies commitment to values.

Modern British religious education has all the marks of a 'carrier of modernity' and it is not surprising that these tensions are felt keenly by all those concerned with it. The churches and the other religious communities, although confronted by modernity and existing within it, are not in the same sense to be regarded as carriers of it. This is why commitment as seen by the religious education teacher is subtly different from commitment as seen by the priest or minister of religion. The language of commitment as spoken by these two professions has, in recent years, been spoken with different accents.

The exploration of commitment and values presents a number of unresolved tensions in contemporary religious education.

Religion, Ideology and Education

May 1974

Education is not a neutral activity but is laden with values. There is a sense in which education may thus be regarded as an ideology. Does not the claim that religions and ideologies should be critically examined in education come to grief on the claim that education itself is necessarily ideological? Surely not, for the argument is not against religion or ideology as such, but against dogmatic religion and closed, authoritarian ideologies. If education is an ideology, it is certainly an open and critical ideology, which is why it finds support from the critical, enquiring strands which are to be found in all major religions.

There is a tension between education on the one hand and the religions and secular ideologies on the other. Education is critical, sceptical and enquiring. Religion is passionate, committed and adoring. The secular ideologies are passionate, committed and adoring. Moreover, the 'true believer', whether in religion or politics, has an instructional attitude towards those who would learn from him/her. Whether you are being taught by the Maharishi, the Marxists, or the Mormons (what about the Methodists?) what you receive is instruction. You are told the teachings. You are helped to adapt your outlook (as they say) to the doctrine. The instructor assumes the truth of the instruction. It is received on authority, it is written in the book. The manual, whether in the form of the manifesto or the agreed syllabus, is central to instruction. The instructor knows. The pupils do not know. The task is to tell them.

Single instruction

The ideal situation for an instructional religion or ideology is when it alone has possession of the school. Every such religion and ideology seeks to gain control of the schools. The history of the school in Vorster's South Africa, in Mao's China, in Castro's Cuba, in Catholic Spain, in Lutheran Norway, in Islamic Pakistan and in Christian Britain, had this in common: no instruction shall be permitted in the school except in the true faith. This is why the notion of power-sharing in ownership of schools excites such controversy in a highly ideological society such as Northern Ireland. The true believer, when faced with the prospect of losing a grip on the school, instinctively mutters 'relativity'. A school which does not instruct in the true faith must be a school which 'fails to give guidance to young people', which promotes 'uncertainty', or which creates a 'dangerous vacuum'.

Multiple instruction

Multiple instruction is where several religions and ideologies are permitted to offer instruction in their tenets. The authority of an instruction is undermined if it encounters another instruction, so in multiple instruction it is normal to divide pupils according to their faith or their alleged faith or their parents' faith. Instructors are usually nominated by or accredited by or trained by the religion or ideology they represent. Since the religions and ideologies never actually meet, this situation can be called 'parallel instruction'. This sort of situation arises only in a pluralistic democracy – that is, a society in which no one religion or ideology has power and where a citizen can change his allegiance without suffering loss of civil rights or social standing. This situation is not as good from the point of view of the ideologies as a single instruction but it is better than education. At least with multiple instruction, you have a chance to build up your own flock and perhaps gain a few adherents.

Education and dialogue

The task of education, however, is not to proclaim ideologies or religions but to scrutinize them. 'Teachers are to present possible truth for exploration, not actual truth for commitment: if the pupil moves on to faith, his journey must be without more support than would be given to a fellow pupil moving in the opposite direction.' (D. G. Attfield, 'The Justification of Assembly' in *Learning for Living*, May 1974, Vol. 13, No. 5, p. 175). Education does not seek to win the assent of the pupil to any given teaching but only co-operation in the enquiry. Its main aim is to help pupils go on learning.

Why there must be religious education

The change from instruction to education is not proving to be an easy one for the religions. The secular or non-religious stances for living, if they enter the religious curriculum in any significant way, will not find it easy either. Naturally, all teaching must be sensitive and tactful. One must always teach as if in the presence of the believer whose faith is being described and one must allow the believer a significant voice when deciding if the description is accurate or not. This is not the same as being free to instruct without rivals and without restraint.

This task is surely one of the most significant duties of the school in a pluralistic democracy. Unless approached in this way, there can be no treatment at all in the school of these controversial values and beliefs. We would then have a silent school, a school which hid from its pupils the great faiths by which people live, for which they struggle and die, a school which offers no information, no clarification, no preparation for responsible life in a society where these things are debated. Then indeed we would have a vacuum, and the school would fall prey to those in whose interest it is that young people should become unreflective consumers.

Missing the point

The secularists who argue (as only a few still do) that there should be no religious education in school are missing the point about education in a democracy. Why should religion escape the open questioning of young people in school? The Christians who are alarmed about the introduction of courses in communism are also missing the point. Why should communism be exempt from the descriptive dialogue which the classroom offers? It cannot be said too frequently: the spirit of education is hostile to all totalitarianism, whether of the right or the left, and to all instructional mentalities, whether religious or secular.

A tension but not a breaking point

The relationship between the religions and ideologies and the spirit of education is thus one of some tension. But it is a tension within a unity; it can be a creative tension, not an absolute antagonism. There are forms of Christian and Muslim faith which encourage this view of education. The same is true of humanism. Some true believers, whether religious or secular, are learning that they are no less true to their faith because they are willing still to go on learning, even if it means learning from each other. Far from being free of values or neutral with regard to beliefs, this critical, enquiring, liberating, descriptive, rational, personal and ethical form of religious education arises precisely as an expression of the values which belong to human beings, not as Marxist, humanist, Hindu or Christian, but human beings as such. Any religion or ideology which can find within these values some which it holds dear will not, in the end, conclude that education has betrayed it.

Chapter 2

Religious Education: Problems and Methods

Everybody engaged in religious education in British schools must grapple with the relationship between the vocation and practice of teaching religion and the question of personal religious faith. In this article, an attempt was made to deal with this problem by using the vocabulary of divergence and convergence. The basic idea is that a religious believer may be prompted by the nature of the religious commitment to present religion critically in a pluralistic context, while on the other hand there are also forms of religious commitment in which teaching is most naturally concentrated upon transmission or replication of the faith of the teacher. Of course, there are many teachers of religious education who although interested in the study of religion do not have personal faith of their own. The following extract does not deal with their situation, but is concerned only with the way in which the teacher who does have a personal faith can relate that faith to the teaching of religious education today.

Commitment and the teacher of religion

This vexed question is still much discussed in British religious education. But the vocabulary of the debate and the distinctions which are used are seldom satisfactory. It has been common to distinguish between the teachers of religion who allow their personal faith to colour their presentation, and those who keep their own religious faith (if they have one) firmly out of the classroom. The latter is sometimes thought of as being the more professional type of teacher, while the former has been called 'confessionalist'. This is, however, an unhappy distinction, for it does not offer any way for the teacher of religion who does have personal religious faith to find a unity between faith and work which will be educationally acceptable. The distinction between confessional and professional has done more to muddy the waters of the debate about commitment than anything else. We need a new vocabulary which will enable us to preserve the distinction between educational and uneducational ways of teaching religion in county schools, but will at the same time avoid relegating the personal religious faith of the teacher to the private sphere. We must, at the same time, preserve the legitimacy of the situation (which we find more and more in British religious education) in which the plurality of the teaching force as a whole is reflected in the range of religious and non-religious views held by RE teachers. The RE teacher need not have religious faith, but if he or she does have religious faith, it need not be excluded from the classroom, provided that it can give rise to educational teaching and not be expressed through preaching or fostering one religion rather than another.

Divergent and convergent teaching

Perhaps the ideas of being divergent and convergent will supply what is needed. Divergent teachers are those whose personal faith may not be the same as the content of their teaching and their hopes and expectations for the development of their pupils. Convergent teachers, on the other hand, are those in whose lives these three elements converge; i.e. personal religious faith, a preference for teaching it, and the hope that their pupils will come to share it.

One advantage of talking like this is that whereas it was a 'bad thing' to be confessional and a 'good thing' to be professional, divergence and convergence are descriptive terms which do not present evaluations of this kind. The teacher working with the churches in parish education would be perfectly professional in being convergent, while the RE teacher in the county school would be professional in being divergent. Another advantage of using this distinction is that the way is cleared for seeing that personal religious faith can be expressed in either a divergent or a convergent way, in that a teacher who teaches religions which do not command his/her personal commitment may nevertheless do so because of the incentive which his or her own personal religious faith offers. The very divergency may thus be the expression of religious commitment, and so in a sense may be thought of as a kind of confessionalism, but one which is educational. In the case of certain kinds of personal religious faith, causing pupils to consider other religions may have as much immediate impact in the classroom as (in the case of another kind of religious faith) causing pupils to become adherents of your own faith may have.

A religious faith which leads to educational teaching

Convergence is easy to understand. Everyone expects religious people to want to help others towards their own faith. But why should a religious person want people to *question* his or her own faith and to learn from other religions? The situation of the divergent teacher, although his or her religious faith may affect his or her classroom work as much as the convergent teacher's work is affected, is less simple and obvious.

The answer lies, as hinted already, in the kind of religion to which the teacher is committed. It is sometimes said that religions provide answers to ultimate questions. This is a half truth. Religions provide perspectives and frames of reference within which the asking of ultimate questions becomes imperative. The teacher whose personal religious faith leads him or her to divergent teaching will be the one for whom every religious answer leads to further questions, and whose religion thus pushes him or her into a life of criticism and enquiry.

The RE teacher's main resource?

It has been suggested that the personal religious faith of the teacher should be his or her teaching resource. There may be some limited truth in this, although it must be qualified by the counter-claim that the main resource of the religious education teacher should be professional training and one's own experience and skill as a teacher. Whether there is even a limited truth in the claim depends on whether it is to be taken in a convergent or a divergent manner. If the suggestion is that the teachers' own religion should be their main resource in the sense that they will teach their own religion and will seek to perpetuate it in their pupils, they would be convergent. There is no place for the convergent teacher in the state schools of a pluralist democracy. But if the idea is that their personal religion will be of the kind which will thrust them into enquiry and will thus enable them to be divergent and thus fully educational in the sense required for state-school religious education, then the claim may often be true. While there is a place in religious education for the teacher whose teaching is inspired by nothing but concern for children and interest in religious studies, there is also a great need for teachers whose educational treatment of religion in the classroom stems from the critical impulse provided by their own commitment to a critical faith.

Religious Education and Identity

Spring 1991

A popular sound bite on the part of politically conservative commentators on religious education is that 'multi-faith leads to no faith'. However, there is little if any evidence to support this claim. Indeed, many careful and experienced teachers of world religions working with quite young children find that the religious identity of the child is confirmed and strengthened by a sympathetic encounter with other faiths. In that case, what is the appeal of the slogan 'multi-faith means no faith'? It seems to spring from certain assumptions about the nature of identity and the nature of the contribution which the study of world religions may make to the formation of the child's identity. These are the questions discussed in the following extract.

Does religious education confuse children?

In his pioneering work on identity, Erik H. Erikson has shown that adolescence is the critical period in the life-cycle for the formation of identity. Erikson contrasts identity formation with identity confusion or diffusion. This suggests that behind the question about religious education and confusion lies the deeper question about religious education and identity. Confusion, we might think, is the opposite of identity.

In forging an identity, the adolescent does not work with nothing. All of the relative and partial identifications formed during earlier childhood may now be called upon. The impact of significant other people will be important, and so will the contribution to be made by political and religious groups to which the adolescent might now belong.

The problem for the teacher is to distinguish between creative confusion, which might be a constructive contribution to later identity, and destructive confusion. For example, although identity is characteristically formed during adolescent years, tough-minded religious socialisation may produce precocious identity formation in quite young children. A number of psychological studies have shown that if this happens in the life of the ten-year-old child, little scope is found for the inclusion of sexuality into identity, and the precocious identity formation will often break up suddenly later in life under the impact of a sexual crisis. Such sexual breakdowns are rather common in religious communities where great emphasis is placed upon securing the religious conversion of young children before the onset of puberty in order to protect them from adolescent sexuality.

The foreclosure of the quest for identity can lead to a lack of creativity in personal life, and we may say that education is just as interested in contributing to flexible and enquiring personalities as it is in the formation of fixed identities. Moreover, since ideologies (including political and religious ones) help to form identity, might it not be the case that identity itself is an ideological concept? Powerful religions and political philosophies do have a tendency to act like magnets on people's lives, creating clear patterns and, perhaps, rigid ones, but this is not necessarily in the interests of the most mature community and individual development.

Sources of confusion

It might help us to distinguish between creative and destructive confusion if we examine a little more closely the kinds of classroom experience which are sometimes said to be confusing for children. Immediately, a striking fact emerges: what is said to be confusing is almost always the teaching of world religions. This is a surprising discovery, because on the face of it an approach through the religions of the world should be no more confusing than any other approach in religious education. The Bible, for example, is a complex book, and anyone who has studied the relationships between the synoptic gospels might well feel confused. Christianity is a large and complex faith, and anyone who studies the contradictory opinions of Christians on almost any subject might also feel confused. Strangely enough, the fear that children will be confused never seems to arise from the teaching of the Bible and Christianity but only from the teaching of world religions. This underlines clearly the contribution which religious education is expected to make to the formation of identity, and identity is conceived as falling within the domain of a particular religion. To draw identity from more than one religion would be to form a synchronistic identity, and that would be thought undesirable.

The educational task

The belief that children are confused by the teaching of world religions implies a connection between teaching and the formation of religious identity which must be questioned. One of the central characteristics of education is the wide perspective which it offers. Education is concerned to create flexible personalities, to form people with the courage of their own convictions and sufficient confidence to mix easily in any walk of life. An important part in this process is played by the range of materials which should be presented to children and young people. It is precisely this range and diversity that the school, with its hundreds of pupils, its dozens of teachers, its library and its other information retrieval systems, can offer over and above the more limited circle of the family. Is the educational perspective of religious education to be replaced by denominational instruction, and all for the sake of something which is not the proper concern of religious education in the county schools in the first place?

Distinguishing educational confusion from identity confusion

It is significant that the source of confusion in the teaching of world religions is usually attributed to the thematic approach. On straightforward educational grounds, however, there is no reason why thematic teaching should be any more confusing than presenting religions one by one. Topics such as death, marriage or green issues are both relevant and intelligible. The mere fact that they are illustrated by examples drawn from several religions in no way diminishes this. Teaching which is poorly organized and badly presented will certainly confuse pupils, and it is this educational confusion which we should obviously avoid.

Nevertheless, although it is not part of its purpose, a truly educational religious education may contribute to the formation of religious identity. The distinctiveness of one family background is emphasized when its difference from others is realized. For many children, awareness of belonging to a particular religious tradition is heightened not so much in the home where it is taken for granted but in the school. Under the guidance of sympathetic teachers, such an awareness can strengthen and confirm the child's feeling of solidarity with his or her family's religious community. In the case of older young people, it remains true that only those religious identities chosen in the knowledge of alternatives are likely to remain firm as young people leave schools and colleges for work or further study away from home. Children cannot forever be protected from wider horizons and challenging alternatives. The religious education teacher who can present these thoughtfully in a curriculum which both reflects Christianity and takes account of other religions will serve the pupils well.

Religious Education and the Quest for Meaning

Winter 1980

This item continues the discussion about the relationship between religion and education, particularly in so far as the religious commitment of the teacher is concerned. The first section in this chapter outlined the differences between the teacher with divergent faith and the one with convergent faith. In the present section, a similar problem is discussed, taking our starting point from the idea that religious education can be considered as a contribution to the quest for meaning on the part of the pupil.

It is often said that religious education contributes to the quest for the meaning in life. Indeed, the making of meaning is often thought of as one of the major goals of religious education, and one of the reasons why religion is taught in schools.

There certainly are some advantages in thinking of religious education in this way. Much contemporary humanistic psychology and psychotherapy emphasizes the importance for personality development of maintaining a view of life which sees it as purposeful and meaningful. One thinks of the work of Victor Frankl and his 'logotherapy'. In as much as the search for meaning in life seems to be a fundamental human need, this emphasis has enabled religious education to see itself as a principal part of a liberal, child-centred education based on humanitarian values but not necessarily dependent on the particular claims of any one religion. The emphasis upon meaning has thus made it possible for religious education to move from its traditional faith-fostering role whilst retaining its concern for the general nurture of the whole pupil.

This approach has also had important consequences for the religious education curriculum which, in the infant and middle school, has been able to relate much ordinary and secular life experience to specific religious topics in theme teaching. Religion has been seen as offering a total interpretation of life. In the secondary school such matters as the quest for personal identity and a wide range of personal and social problems have similarly been legitimized as part of religious education. The 'meaning of life' approach has also incorporated the study of world religions since these can be looked upon as more or less coherent sets of 'answers' to the basic 'questions' which are posed or implied by much ordinary human experience.

However, there are limits to the usefulness of the argument that religious education contributes to the pupils' quest for meaning, and the approach may be misleading if it is exaggerated.

The limits of RE as 'meaning-making'

One of the weaknesses of the approach is that it claims for religious education something which is really the task of the whole curriculum. This can be seen by some teachers as an attempt on the part of religious education to take over the curriculum. The truth is that every subject has its contribution to make to the child's growing interpretation of life and although religious education is particularly self-conscious about the values inherent within its subject matter this is probably not a distinction which religious educators should seek for their subject. Rather, each subject should be encouraged to explore its own values and commitments, and to present itself to the pupils as having a contribution to make to their quest for beauty and significance in living.

Moreover, if religious education is looked upon as the sole agency of meaning-making in school, intolerable strains are imposed upon it. It then begins to be asked whether, in offering itself as the subject concerned with the meaning of life but in confining its 'answers' to those provided by religions, religious education is not showing itself to be unbalanced or unfair or prejudiced in favour of religion. The absurdity of supposing that it is a mark of bias in a subject for it to concentrate upon its own content is soon seen if it is clearly emphasized that the proper content of religious education is religion and not the whole question of the meaning of life. The 'answers' offered by religions are to be balanced against the 'answers' offered by the sciences, the arts and the other humanities. While the question of 'balance' and 'bias' *within* religious studies is a matter of concern for religious educators, the problem of 'fairness' in dealing with the meaning of life *as a whole* is a problem for curriculum planners and involves the whole staff of the school. It is probably true that some focus is needed for this concern for the whole meaning of life and for the deeper values of the curriculum, but this central focus is most naturally to be found not in classroom religious education but in the school assembly.

Do religions ask questions or offer answers?

Another misleading aspect of the approach to religious education which over-emphasizes its role as contributing to the quest for meaning in life is the image of religion which this over-emphasis presents. The 'questions' are seen as having their origin in natural aspects of human life: our human vulnerability to pain, death and guilt, the fragility of life, and the limits of our power over nature. The religions, on the other hand, are seen as offering 'answers' to these problems; answers which are speculative and controversial and are yet offered or even asserted with confidence. The task of religious education is thus to compare one set of answers with another. In this strange and unrealistic

43

division of question and answer the critical and enquiring impulse is located in the human spirit itself or in the stimulus posed by the situation of people in the world, while the religions, although proceeding from this universal and natural level, are conceived of as the response rather than the stimulus. This division conceives of philosophy as enquiring, and theology as dogmatizing. People ask why; God tells them.

Perhaps religion is often like this. No doubt the resurgence of fundamentalist and intolerant religious enthusiasm can be interpreted as the reaction of puzzled people seeking a simple security in religion, but religion need not be like this, and the distinction we have been discussing completely fails to understand a central feature of much religion – namely, the *way* it *raises* questions.

It is belief in the goodness and power of God which makes the pain and evil in the world seem puzzling. It is belief in the justice of God and in the moral seriousness of human actions which makes it seem intolerable that death should be the end. For the collectivist, whether of the Marxist or humanist evolutionary kind, the difficulty in explaining and defending the value of the particular individual is no difficulty, for the individual is subordinate to the group, but for the Christian, Jew or Muslim committed to belief in a particular God, knowing and caring for concrete individuals becomes imperative. These are simply a few examples of the way in which religious belief offers a frame of reference in which, while certain problems are resolved, others are opened up. This leads to a characteristic feature of the intellectual life of the religious thinker. The impulse for critical enquiry comes directly from faith. It is not conceived of as providing a challenge *to* faith coming from *beyond* faith, but is a product of faith itself. In the quest for meaning in life, religion is not only part of the answer; it is part of the problem.

Critical faith and the divergent teacher

This point is of importance not only for the way in which the task of religious education in making a contribution to people's quest for meaning is understood, but also for understanding the nature of the relationship between the religious faith (should he or she have one) of the religious education teacher and one's work as a professional educator. Let us return to the distinction between the convergent teacher and the divergent teacher. The former describes teachers who teach their own faith, in order to further increase the interests of their own faith, and the latter describes those who *because of their faith* teach a variety of faiths seeking to further the interests of none. But teachers who think of religion as only giving answers or who find that in their own religious life religion gives answers while life presents problems can hardly be expected to understand the position of the divergent teacher. They will not understand how one can teach a variety of faiths *because of* one's commitment to a single faith, because they will not understand how religion itself, the more one is committed to it, becomes the stimulus for constant enquiry. In that case, however, convergent teachers will not understand the connection between religion and education. They will not be able to work their way from their religious commitment to their role as educators. They will either cease to be true educators or will leave their religious commitment outside the classroom, priding themselves on their professionalism.

Diagnosis

It is not difficult for a teacher of religion with religious commitment to tell whether his or her commitment is of the convergent or the divergent kind. Does your faith have for you a 'discovery' quality? Do the answers which your faith provides for you lead you on to further questions? Do you find that your obedience and your questioning escalate together and because of one another?

The quest for a truly open religious education is by no means over. It is true that the nature of such an 'educational religious education' must be defended on educational grounds. But a closed religion is no ally for an open education. When the claims of an open religious education can be supported by an enquiring model of education and also by an enquiring model of religion we shall have a rationale for the subject which will be more coherent, educationally more sound, and religiously more satisfying.

Normal Science, Normal Religion and the Problem of Meaning

Autumn 1990

With the introduction of the National Curriculum in 1988, technology became a required subject in both primary and secondary schools. This stimulated a good deal of discussion about the spiritual and human values of technology and in 1990 the BJRE *published a special issue on this subject. The following text formed the introduction to this special issue.*

Research in particle physics is becoming much more expensive. The point seems to have been reached where the cost of the new technology required to extend the research capability is disproportionate to the significance and the usefulness of what might be discovered. As the military significance of fundamental research diminishes, it seems unlikely that governments will have the political will to divert funds from industrial development and social uses to supply the needs of basic research in this and other related scientific areas.

Faced with this difficulty in creating new research programmes, many research scientists will be attracted to reviewing existing research data. This will lead to new theoretical speculation about the best interpretation of the data, and will encourage some scientists with a metaphysical inclination to create big theories. At their most comprehensive, these big theories will tend to become cosmic, mystical and even religious.

It is during times of technological and financial crisis that normal science drifts towards an examination of meaning. It is almost twenty years now since Thomas Kuhn described the nature of 'normal science' as being enclosed within the borders of routine experimentation in which the general theoretical framework is mainly taken for granted.

Normal religion is not much different from normal science. When we say that religion is a quest for meaning, that is certainly not true for most religious people. If at some point in a person's life religion offered answers to life's problems, the normal religious believer has long since forgotten that there were answers and problems. The normal religious life is lived in a routine way, against a framework of ethical, social and emotional factors which are almost entirely taken for granted. It is in times of crisis that religion, like science, tends to become contemplative. In religion this will seldom if ever take the form of a technological and financial frustration, but will generally be the result of an increase in cognitive dissonance when the taken-for-granted framework of the religious life is challenged. This may take place when other religious groups make contact, thus heightening awareness of a religious world-view which can no longer be taken for granted. Normal religion now either retreats into protective enclaves or becomes involved in dialogue or mission.

It is the encounter between modernity as a whole and religion which has created the modern religious quest for meaning. It is not only the encounter between world religions, or between religions and their secular counterparts, but modernity as such which has challenged religious normality. Modernity creates mobility of persons, things and ideas. Modernity is intimately involved with novelty. Modernity forces religious spirituality to modify itself to the demands of an industrial society, and ultimately religious spirituality becomes aware of this modification.

Revolutionary science makes problems for normal religion, just as revolutionary religion makes problems for normal science. The history of the relationships between science and religion shows cases of many types. This encounter will produce problems of mutual meaning, and the handling of this meaning will be a crucial part of the survival of a science and a religion which have become self-conscious in their various world-views. Recent developments in cognitive stage theory throw considerable light on the different ways in which the problems of meaning in the two spheres are related. Relationships between science and religion become interesting for education when there is something the teacher can do about them. Cognitive theory helps us to see that there is a pedagogical approach, a way of teaching, a style of discussion, which is appropriate to children and young people at various ages and stages of growth. In this way, the relationship between science and religion yields not only content for curriculum development but also methods appropriate for each stage.

The religious education response

It would seem too simple to claim that the task of religious education is to integrate the problems of science and religion. This would be to prejudge the situation, and would lead to a religious education which was excessively defensive on behalf of religion. In handling the balance between two kinds of world views, disintegration may be as important as integration. It may be just as important to know when things will not mix, that mixing would be inappropriate, as to realize that there are unexpected ways in which they might be brought together. Teachers of both science and religion need to know when it is appropriate to bring together and when to hold apart. Above all, it is the role of both subjects to ensure that they rise above the level of normality. The uncritical science teacher, aware of everyone's ideology except his or her own cannot be a good teacher of science, but at best an instructor in 'normal' science. In the same way, the teacher of religion who never realizes that religious views may have to be modified and not merely commended must also be considered a poor teacher, however faithful in his or her normal religion.

Beyond meaning

The encounter between science and religion will seldom go beyond questions of mutual meaning. Problems of meaning usually occur in the realm of ideas. They arise as a result of cognitive dissonance, which is the clash between various ways of knowing, or things that are known. Problems of meaning occur in people's minds, and although an unsolved problem of meaning may be disturbing and even physically destructive, it is primarily mental.

The 1988 Education Reform Act requires a broad and a balanced curriculum which will contribute to the development not only of the mental but also of the spiritual and the moral. There is a tendency for classical, liberal education with its commitment to rationality to remain at the mental level, and religious education may easily succumb to this tendency. Theories of cognitive development are obviously concerned with mental functioning and however significant these are for the teaching processes, religious education must rise beyond the mental to the spiritual and the moral.

A reading of the first chapter of the Gospel of John shows us that in at least one classic religious text one rises beyond the mental by sinking into the body, for 'the word was made flesh'. It is here that the debate between science and religion turns into the debate between religion and technology.

Technology is to do with people's bodies. Technology makes scientific principles active by bringing new forces into play with human bodies. While science has to do with questions of meaning, technology has to do with human pain and pleasure. It is new technology which packages our food, heals our wounds and turns part of our globe into a village. Of course, technology has an intimate relationship with experimental science, since it has to do with the making of instruments, but technology of the widespread, cultural kind we experience today is not driven primarily by the needs of research science. It is driven by the needs of our economy, by the market place. The market is the place of pleasure and pain, since it is the place where bread and water, stocks and shares, embryos and kidneys are bought and sold.

The question for religious education

'... those who do not love a brother or sister whom they have seen, cannot love God whom they have not seen' (1 John 4:20). Love is not mainly an idea. The relationship between religion and technology should go beyond questions of meaning to a mutual criticism of responsibility for human pleasure and pain. Technology can offer enormous increases of creativity and dignity to disabled people. It also pollutes the air we breathe and the very ground upon which we walk. If the telephone can be divine in overcoming distance between those who are far apart, the television set can be demonic in creating distance between those who are close together.

This two-edged quality can also be seen in religion. Religion drives people into prejudice and neurosis; religion also empowers human beings for divine acts of self-sacrifice.

In its dialogue with science and with technology, religious education encounters the mind and the body of modern human beings. Through intellectual criticism and through challenging the imagination and engaging the emotions, it must move young people beyond the obvious, beyond routine, into a struggle against meaninglessness. By drawing upon the religious heritage of criticism and images, it must also educate young people into responsible management of technology in a world where there is pain. In spite of the colossal accumulation of wealth which has been built up in the Western World through technology, children are still starving. No series of attainment targets which fails to take this fact with the utmost seriousness can be faithful to the character of religion.

Religious Education and Personal, Social and Moral Education

Spring 1988

The search for a viable philosophy of religious education has moved from the question of whether religion can offer meaning and purpose to young people to the question of whether the 'study of' religion can offer something. In religious education, the religions are not confronted directly, but through the process of education. In 1987 Michael Grimmitt's great book Religious Education and Human Development *had appeared, and a group of religious educators in Birmingham were beginning to create a way of teaching religious education to young children which was justified not because it enabled the child to understand religion but because it enabled religion, or religious education to put it more precisely, to give its gifts of human development to children. This is the complex of questions which the following article seeks to unravel.*

What is the contribution of religious education to personal, social and moral education?

Whatever the answer to this important question, it must be clearly understood that religious education teachers should not think of decreasing the number of periods which involve specific religious content and changing over to lessons which involve personal, moral or social materials without reference to religion. Religious education may be fulfilled through PSME but it must not be sacrificed to it. If it is thought desirable that time during school hours should be made available for a non-religious PSME, and if it is expected that religious education departments in secondary schools should be responsible for this or should have a significant role in it, then *additional* timetable periods must be provided.

PSME is the responsibility of the whole curriculum

It will, however, probably not be necessary to think of increasing the number of periods available to religious education simply in order to make it possible for religious education departments to undertake non-religious PSME, since it is surely the responsibility of the entire curriculum to contribute to the personal, moral and social development of pupils. If teachers in all primary and secondary schools were more fully aware of the responsibility which each and every school subject carried in this respect, there would be less danger of a misguided emphasis upon religious education. It would, moreover, enable us to focus attention upon the central question, which is how the study of world religions may contribute to the development of the pupil.

This does not mean a mono-religious approach

There is, in Britain, a traditional connection between the study of Christianity, Christian nurture and the personal, moral and social development of pupils. It was the breakdown of that association in the 1970s which led to the disassociation of moral education from religious education, a disassociation barely disguised in many cases under the distinction between the explicit study of religion and the implicit study of religion, the latter often being little more than the non-religious development of PSME. Now that there is renewed interest in the connection between religion and personal development, it must be emphasized that this should be a progressive movement not a regressive one. Between the two world wars there was great educational interest in what was called citizenship, and the contribution of religious education to this was seen in terms of 'Christian citizenship'. Contemporary religious education must, however, continue to take seriously its responsibility within a multi-cultural and multi-faith society and must resist any temptation to fall back into a simple combination of uncontroversial moralizing and semi-Christian folk religion.

'Personal' must not be reduced to 'individual'

It is encouraging that when pupil development is being discussed the usual expression is 'personal, social and moral development'. The importance of the second expression must not be lost. There are four great issues which confront human society today: human rights (including racism and sexism), poverty both at home and abroad, ecology and the bomb. Pupils, when developed socially, do not merely become nicer people. They become responsible in ways appropriate to their age in these four great social issues. What is the contribution of religious education to that process of social maturation?

Religious faith and human learning

It is when the easy answers, based upon misunderstandings, are ruled out that the central challenge of our questions may be seen more clearly. It is easy enough to see how a religion might make an important contribution to the personal, social and moral development of a person when that person becomes a member of the religion in question, when there is a conversion to the religion or a steady nurturing in the faith of that religion from within. It is, of course, widely debated whether or not religion actually does lead to better mental health. Sigmund Freud regarded religion as an infantile fixation often expressed in neurotic behaviour, while C. G. Jung regarded it as essential that adults, to become fully mature, should come to terms with the great religious symbols. Nevertheless, the issues are clear enough even though they remain controversial. A certain set of attitudes, qualities, beliefs and values is encouraged by Islam, and another by Judaism and so on. To some extent, each fosters a different view of the goal of human development. The religions represent the highest point of human differences precisely because they represent the most disciplined and refined forms of spirituality. The high degree of refinement which the religious traditions have reached in the thousands of years of their growth leads today to the high profile of different types of spirituality which the religions tend to foster. Perhaps it is true that in the end the traditions of spirituality begin to converge again. Perhaps it is true that the saints of all the faiths have certain similarities. Nevertheless, for the vast majority of believers the attitudes and values of religious commitment are distinct or even unique.

The problem arises not when one is asking how having faith in a particular religion can contribute to human development but when one asks how *studying* that single religion may do so. Here, the personal, social and moral values of studying, of the teaching and learning process itself, are intermingled with the values which the religion seeks to nurture, or the values which it exhibits to the student. When one speaks, as one must in modern religious education, of studying not one but several religions, the questions become still more interesting. The introduction of many religions not only adds richness to the content itself, but places further emphasis upon the process of study, since the plurality of the religions being studied tends to increase the sense of distance between the pupil and the religion, making it clearer still that the pupil is not being nurtured into religious faith, but is experiencing processes relevant to human development through work at school.

What have religions to teach us?

And who are you, the religions might ask, to ask that question? Who are you, from the alleged vantage point of your pluralistic classroom, to survey the religions and to ask what they can offer? Who are you, with your secular and educational point of view, to suggest that the religions are there for your use, and to contribute to your human development?

It is true that representatives of the religions do sometimes reply in ways like these when asked the educational question. In reply, it must be pointed out that the educational question does not imply that there is some neutral vantage point above and beyond all religions from which the religion can be surveyed. There is, however, a challenge to the religions, in that the right of any one religion or religions as a group to totally enclose the hearts and minds of pupils is denied.

If it is true that education cannot be allowed the luxury of an independent and neutral point from which to criticize everyone, it is equally true that the religions cannot be permitted to maintain a totalitarian hold upon human beings. What we are dealing with in education is a much more subtle negotiation between various forms of consciousness, various degrees of implicit and explicit religious knowledge, and personal meaning at many different stages of development. One can learn a great deal from a religion without being committed to it body, mind and soul, and one can fail to notice a great deal about the religion to which one is actually committed. Real processes of learning do not take place 'inside' religions or 'inside' education. Learning takes place inside people. In that human region within, there is seldom absolute commitment or absolute educational secularity, but mostly various shades of awareness, sensitivities, doubts, hopes, imagination, traditional expectations and customs, yearnings and all the rest of it. This is what it is actually like in the real lives of the children and young people to whom religious education is presented. What then have our pupils to learn from religion?

Meaning can only be drawn from the spiritual traditions

The German social philosopher Jurgen Habermass has argued in his influential 1973 book *Legitimation Crisis* that the uneasy alliance between the powerful central state and the international industrial company is a characteristic feature of our late-capitalist Western societies. Habermass remarks that this impressive alliance of power and money can do almost anything in our world today except provide people with meaningful lives. The only source of meaning, he argues, are the ancient spiritual traditions. One of the crucial dilemmas of our societies is the way in which they tend to destroy the spiritual traditions and yet, at the same time, without the sustenance of these spiritualities they themselves are bound to fall into deeper and deeper crisis because they will generate meaninglessness.

If it is taught in a way which is relevant to modern spirituality, it is hard to see how any school subject could be more significant, both in the short run and the long run, than religion.

This does not mean that only religious people can be good, and it is not the task of religious education to make pupils good. Religious education is important in the curriculum because it is the main focus for transcendence. The questions which our pupils ask of religion are important, but even more significant are the questions which spirituality asks of them. What matters is not only that they question, but that they are questioned. In the whole curriculum young people are encouraged to search for meaning. It is only in religious education that the possibility arises of there being meaning in search of them.

Religious Education and Religionism

Spring 1992

This article was my first attempt to define religionism. Since then I have published a number of additional studies on this question, including: 'A critique of Christian religionism in recent British education' in Jeff Astley and Leslie J. Francis (eds), Christian Theology and Religious Education: connections and contradictions (London, SPCK, 1996, pp. 140–65); 'The theology of the Department for Education' in Educational Review (Vol. 47, No. 3, November 1995, pp. 243–53); The Holy Trinity and Christian Education in a pluralist world (London, National Society/Church House Publishing, 1995); 'Religionism and religious education' in Mal Leicester and Celia Modgil (eds), Values in Education and Cultural Diversity (Cassell, forthcoming).

....

In the year 778 C.E., Charlemagne led his first expedition into Spain against the Moors. In the Pyrenees his rearguard was attacked with heavy loss of life. The incident became the subject of The Song of Roland, which evolved during the period of the Crusades when hostility between Christian and Muslim was at its height. Roland became the symbol of Christian heroism struggling against Islam.

These are the historical traditions and legends which continue to feed the spirit of religious prejudice. A striking example of this may be found in The Song of Roland in the Legacy Library (No. 7) published in London by Frederick Muller Ltd in 1962. Other items in the series deal with Jason and the Golden Fleece, the Adventures of Ulysses, the Arthurian Legends and so on. It is a well-established series frequently found in school libraries.

Religious issues are prominent right from the start of the book about Roland. The Muslim leader, King Marsile, sends a deputation from his court in Saragossa to Charlemagne. ' "We salute you," said their spokesman, "in the name of the glorious God Almighty." Roland, who had moved closer to the emperor, let out a murmur of suspicion at this, but the messenger went on, "Yes, we have decided that your God is the right one. We are ready to worship Him." Now, this was a lie. Roland was right to doubt their words. Marsile and his people were still what the Christians called infidels, or unbelievers. They had made an idol of the prophet Mahomet and worshipped him along with other heathen gods, and they really had no idea at all of giving them up and accepting the Christian God' (page 4).

The treacherous Baron Ganelon, step-father of Roland, and King Marsile prepare a trap for Roland. This treachery was sworn by Ganelon on his sword and by Marsile on the 'Book of Mahomet' (page 12). The plot succeeds, and now we find Roland and his companion in arms, Oliver, together with an archbishop, twelve French peers of the realm and their troops cornered by an overwhelming army of Muslims. 'On his noble charger Veillantis Roland swept forward, open-faced and laughing. A gold-fringed white banner waved skyward from the tip of his lance. He was well-built, and arms became him. He glowered at the Saracens, but when he turned to his own men his look was all of love and humility. He spoke to them courteously' (page 22). The Saracens are, however, described in quite different terms. 'The King, who dealt in black magic, then had his try, with no better luck. The Archbishop, who had strong feelings about pagans in general, went into a rage at the remarks of this particular infidel.' A terrible battle follows. 'All over the field the triple coats of mail of the Saracens and their embroidered shields and jewelled helmets were being smashed and smeared with gore, until all but two of the pagan leaders had been killed' (page 24). 'It was the Archbishop who opened the fray. A Saracen named Abisme came forward carrying a standard with a dragon on it. He was a hateful, gloomy man and the Archbishop loathed him at sight. "That," he said to himself, "is the kind of heathen I never could abide."' (page 29). As the brave Christians attack, the Saracens are soon dying on every side. ' "The curse of Mahomet on France!" the pagans groaned.' 'By God's grace, the Christians triumphed again' and when the Muslim king Marsile hears that his troops have been defeated he is astonished. 'Outside, his people turned in anger against their gods. "Vile gods!" they cried. "So this is how you pay us for our services, with shame and the ruin of our king!" ... then the French took over the city and made them all become Christians' (page 52).

The text of the book is supported by pictures in which handsome red cross knights are shown in battle with evil-looking foreigners, wearing turbans and slippers with pointed tips.

In view of the Gulf War and the ancient resentments which it has aroused, it is most unfortunate that a work of this kind is still to be found on the shelves of school libraries. Not only does it show Europe and the Middle East locked in a religious conflict, but its descriptions of Muslims and Islam are both inaccurate and offensive. Its impact upon the attitudes of both Christian and Muslim young people can only be imagined.

Religionism

We need a new word to describe the attitude toward religion which is encouraged by books of this kind. 'Religionism' might serve the purpose. Religionism describes an adherence to a particular religion which involves the identity of the adherent so as to support tribalistic or nationalistic solidarity. The identity which is fostered by religionism depends upon rejection and exclusion. We are better than they are. We are orthodox; they are infidel. We are believers; they are unbelievers. We are right; they are wrong. The other is identified as the pagan, the heathen, the alien, the stranger, the invader, the one who threatens us and our way of life. Religion is in principle universal in its outlook but religionism is committed to the partial.

Religionism always involves prejudice against other religions. The expression 'religious prejudice' is not, however, sufficient to describe the phenomenon in question, because prejudice is a psychological matter. There is a distinction between racism and racial prejudice. Racism may exist in institutions where individuals have no conscious racial prejudice. Racism may be built up in historical experience, in economic and industrial structures and in international affairs. Although prejudice may be a significant part of racism, to reduce racism to nothing but prejudice is to seriously misunderstand the power and meaning of racism.

The same is true of religion, religious prejudice and religionism. Religionism is present in institutions, in ideologies, in the relationship between entire cultures. It has social and historical roots. Religious prejudice is but a small part of it. Religionism falls as a shadow upon the heart and mind of the individual in the form of religious prejudice, but its structures go beyond the individual.

Religionist tendencies in religious faith

For various complex reasons, it seems to be difficult for religions to evolve without taking on religionist tendencies. Christianity had already assumed a religionist attitude towards Judaism before the close of the New Testament period, and these religionist attitudes were entrenched by the second century. Islam took on religionist features in its emergence from both Christianity and Judaism. Protestantism gathered religionist features during its early struggle with Catholicism. When reforming movements encounter opposition, they attack in order to defend themselves. These attacks quickly adopt caricature and stereotype as their weapons, and the hearts and minds of the second generation of reformers are nurtured within an identity-protecting cocoon, the outer rim of which is hardened by these stereotypes, so religious reform turns into religionism, and evangelism takes on religionist features. As the theology of a religion evolves under such pressures, religionist elements may be built into the very structure, to the point where the deconstruction will be resisted in the name of the integrity of the religious tradition itself.

Anti-religionist education

Just as special educational techniques exist in order to combat racism, so we need a special educational programme to combat religionism. Such programmes of anti-religionist training should become a part of adult education in every church and parish. Such programmes are equally necessary for adults involved in the life of mosques, temples and synagogues. The degree to which it is successfully anti-religionist should become one of the criteria for the evaluation of a new agreed syllabus.

It is not enough for religious education to encourage a tolerant attitude towards other religions. Just as religionism goes beyond religious prejudice so anti-religionist education goes beyond the mere encouragement of tolerance. What is necessary is the deconstruction of the religious consciousness and its theological structure so as to reveal religionist features, isolate them and overcome them by the genuinely religious features of the spiritual tradition. It is particularly important to help religious adults to distinguish between genuinely religious mission and activities which are merely religionist.

The problem of classical literature

The example of *The Song of Roland* which we have discussed leads us into difficult questions about the role of much classical literature. Are we no longer to study Homer because of the hostility towards those who are not Greek? Are we to avoid stories of the saints of the Celtic and Anglo-Saxon churches because of their implied hostility towards the Vikings, now our Scandinavian friends? Are we to avoid the Bible because, here and there, it implies hostility towards those who are not Israelites, or those who are not Christians?

There is no easy answer to these questions. In the first place, however, we must not deny the truth of history. There is a limit to which one can introduce expurgated versions of these classics without fundamentally changing their message. We must also remember that not all the truth lies with us and our generation; the great classics judge us just as we judge them. Nevertheless, we may often be most faithful to the memory of people who went before us by not projecting back into their struggles the conflicts of our own day. We have seen how under the impact of the Crusades the traditions about Roland had already been reshaped. It is not just a question of our generation versus the classics, but the classics already contain the conflict between their own generations and those that came before them.

School libraries and religious education

When we consider the impact of school libraries upon the religious attitudes of our pupils, several principles might be used. First, every school library should have an equal opportunities policy. Old stock should be replaced in the light of this policy. Such a policy should include religionist literature, just as it deals with racist literature and books with a gender-bias. Wherever possible, the stories of the classics retold for children thirty or forty years ago should be replaced by more recent versions. There are today many gifted authors writing for children, and many have successfully reinterpreted the classics, without the naive and overt religionism which is evident in the example we have quoted. Where the work in question is soaked through and through with religionism, it might still be possible to use it provided that the attention of pupils is drawn by the book itself to this feature. Readers should be encouraged to realize that the saga or legend has such features, and should be helped to distance themselves rather than being unconsciously drawn into such attitudes.

At the end of the day, religious education itself should be the most effective antidote against religionism. That will only happen, however, if religious education teachers maintain a critical vigilance both towards their own attitudes and towards those of their resources.

Religious Education and the Spiritual Rights of Children

Summer 1992

In this article an attempt is made to found the spiritual education of children on the United Nations Convention on the Rights of the Child (1989). The argument is then related back to the discussion about religionism and the responsibility of religious education in resisting it.

The United Nations Convention on the Rights of the Child was adopted by the General Assembly on 20th November 1989. It acquired the status of international law in September 1990 and (with a number of minor reservations) was ratified by the United Kingdom early in December the same year. By February 1992 it had been ratified by 109 states.

The Convention recognizes 'the right of every child to a standard of living adequate for the child's physical, mental, spiritual, moral and social development' (Article 27.1). This suggests a number of questions for teachers in Britain. It is noteworthy that in presenting a curriculum which promotes the spiritual, moral, cultural, mental and physical development of the pupil and of society, as required in the 1988 Education Reform Act, the aims of education in this country are fully consistent with the ideals of the Convention. The spiritual rights of the child, however, are located by the Convention not first in the education of the child but in its standard of living. There is a connection between spirituality and poverty. Spirituality, we are thus reminded, is not only to do with the 'spirit' but with the physical well-being of the child. Religious education teachers, insofar as they are concerned to advance the spiritual rights of the child, must be particularly concerned with those children who come to school under-nourished and poorly clothed, from homes struggling to escape the poverty trap. The interest which school governors and headteachers take in the spirituality of their children should be reflected in a greater concern for their physical well-being.

The right to freedom

The Convention affirms 'the right of the child to freedom of thought, conscience and religion' (Article 14.1). The task of education is to promote the freedom of thought of the child. Nothing is more central to freedom of thought than freedom of conscience and of religion. It is particularly important that the rights of children from minority religious groups should be maintained. Moreover, of every syllabus of religious education we should ask whether and how it educates the conscience of the child and develops the child's powers of free thought.

Identity

Having asserted that it is illegal to deprive a child of his or her identity, the Convention asserts that 'where a child is illegally deprived of some or all of the elements of his or her identity, states parties shall provide appropriate assistance and protection, with a view to speedily re-establishing his or her identity' (Article 8.2). What are the responsibilities of religious education in establishing the identity of the child? How can this be reconciled with conferring upon the child the right of freedom of thought? Identity, it would seem, is to be both established and educated, both nourished and challenged. At the very least, this implies a curriculum which confirms the religious identity by placing it within a wider social context, and challenges it by placing it beside other family backgrounds, treated with equal understanding and respect.

The right of free expression

The Convention asserts that it is a duty 'to assure to the child who is capable of forming his or her own views the right to express those views freely in all matters affecting the child, the views of the child being given due weight in accordance with the age and maturity of the child' (Article 12.1). This has an obvious bearing upon teaching method. Children are to be taught in such a way as to advance their maturity in forming their own views and in expressing them. They are not to become mere objects of instruction but are to be developed as expressive and creative agents. The role of discussion and of speech in general is suggested here.

Religious education and values

According to the Convention one of the aims of education is 'the development of respect for the child's parents, his or her own identity, language and values, for the national values of the country in which the child is living, the country from which he or she may originate, and for civilizations different from his or her own' (Article 29.1c). In order to meet this ideal, religious education must be multi-cultural, and this multi-culturalism must be expressed through three focal points. First, the child must be introduced to the values (and these will include the religious values) of the host society. These values will, in the case of the United Kingdom, already be pluralistic and multi-cultural in character. They will be values dependent upon the fact that the principal religious traditions in this country are in the main Christian but there will also be values from the religious traditions of this country which are not, perhaps, to be regarded as 'principal' but which are nevertheless a significant element in the values of British society. To these must be added the teaching and practices and, consequently, the values of the other principal religions represented in this country.

This leads to the second focus, which is upon the values of the society from which the child originates. Origination does not necessarily mean that the child was born elsewhere. Children of the second or third generation of immigrant parents possess an undiminished right to be nurtured and challenged within the values of the society of their origin. If religion is the soul of culture, and if religious education continues to be marginalized under the increasing competition generated by the present interpretation of the National Curriculum, there will be a stronger case for the provision of schools in which religious and cultural values of a specific kind will receive particular encouragement.

The third focus is upon the values of civilizations which are different. This not only points to the difference between the religious values of the family and those of the host society, but to the values of civilizations which may be far removed in space and time from any known to the child. Such perspectives are essential if the role of education is to be fulfilled in enabling children to develop freedom of thought, and to explore their cultural and spiritual heritage. The spiritual rights of the child are not confined to the family or the society but are as large as the household of humanity.

Equality and solidarity

'... the child should be fully prepared to live an individual life in society and brought up ... in the spirit of peace, dignity, tolerance, freedom, equality and solidarity' (Preamble). This is the nearest the Convention comes to a definition of the ingredients of spirituality. The child is to be brought up in the spirit of the following virtues. These virtues are thus to form the spirit or the spirituality into which the child is to be initiated. What is the contribution of religious education in building up the spirituality of peace, dignity and tolerance?

We have argued above for a new programme of religious education which could be described as 'anti-religionist'. By this, we had in mind a programme of training, whether for children or adults, which would be comparable with the anti-racist and anti-sexist training programmes so widely used in schools and industrial companies today. It is unfortunate that a number of religions have built into their belief structure elements of hostility to other religions. These encourage attitudes of superiority, intolerance and imperialism towards members of other faiths. Such attitudes were described as 'religionist' because they promote tribalistic and sectarian religion rather than the religion of peace, dignity and tolerance. Every religious education syllabus should be evaluated as a contribution to anti-religionist training.

The contribution of religious education to equality and solidarity must give us pause for thought. Equality and solidarity are not merely abstract values within religions; they are structural factors in educational systems. As higher education becomes increasingly inaccessible to students from poorer families, it becomes more removed from the ideals of equality and solidarity. In view of the fact that every selection implies a non-selection, the implications of selective education for equality and solidarity demand careful ethical and theological scrutiny by all those concerned with religious values in education. Indeed, a theology of equality and solidarity has a strong claim to be the basis of any relevant theology of education in Britain today.

Spiritual Education and the Money Culture

Summer 1995

This was one of my earliest attempts to expose the spiritual culture which flows from money. My Glasgow lecture 'Spiritual education, religion and the money culture' *had already been published as* 'St Andrews College, occasional papers in education, number 3, 1995'. *This was followed the same year by my lecture for the National Society,* 'The Holy Trinity and Christian education in a pluralist world' *(National Society/Church House Publishing) and the following year by* 'Religious education and the conflict of values in modern Europe' *in Aasulv Lande and Werner Ustorf (eds),* Mission in a pluralist world *(Frankfurt, Peter Lang),* 'Christian education in a capitalist society: Money and God' *in David Ford and Dennis L. Stamps (eds),* Essentials of Christian community, essays in honour of Daniel W. Hardy *(Edinburgh, T & T Clark, pp. 241–52) and* 'The ambiguity of spiritual values' *in J. Mark Halsted and Monica Taylor (eds),* Values in education and education in values *(London, Falmer Press, pp. 33–44). My most recent efforts are:* 'Karl Marx on Capital: Some implications for Christian adult education' *in* Modern Believing *(Vol. 38 No. 1, January 1997, pp. 22–31);* 'Christian education: sufficient or necessary?' *(in two parts) in* Epworth Review *(Vol. 24 Nos 1 & 2, January and April 1997, pp. 40–48 and 38–46);* 'Modernity and Morality: Some issues in the Christian education of adults' *in* Religious Education *(forthcoming).*

Nearly everybody agrees that spirituality is ambiguous, illusive and ill-defined. Various explanations are offered for this. Some say that it is the very nature of the spiritual to be free, spontaneous and indefinable. Sometimes the ambiguity is seen as a decline in standards, as if the firm backbone of values had given way to a kind of jelly-like modernity. Almost everyone agrees, however, that spirituality has to do with basic values in living and hence has to do with the essential nature of education. It is equally clear that education in Britain has never been without a quest for the spiritual, and that this quest has sharpened in intensity in the last couple of years.

Spirituality and the social sciences

Because of its close connection with religious education and the fact that many of those who write about it have a background of theological study, a good deal of the current discussion about spirituality in education approaches the problem from the perspective provided by philosophical anthropology. People speak of a spiritual dimension of personality, or of a spiritual element present in culture and so forth. This is then distinguished in various ways from religion, faith in general or the pursuit of meaning and purpose in living. It might be helpful if the framework of the discussion were grounded in the social sciences. Disciplines such as history, political economy, ideology critique and other cultural studies help us to place spirituality firmly in its context in Britain towards the end of the twentieth century.

Spirituality as a projection of the money culture

A good deal of the spirituality of which people are so conscious today can be regarded as a projection on the ideal plane of forces and realities which lie deeper in society. Much spirituality may thus be regarded as the froth on the surface, or as the attractive veil which obscures the deeper reality. One of the factors which shapes our lives and our values today is undoubtedly money. Money produces its own culture. If we distinguish societies based upon kinship relations, those based upon relations of domination and those based upon money, we can see that in the first the central symbol is blood, in the second it is the sword, while in the third it is money itself. In each type of society, fundamental patterns of human relationship and meaning are determined by the character of the fundamental symbol. Indeed, marriage, military power and money are not merely symbolic of human relationships. They produce and reproduce social relationships modelled upon their own nature.

The money culture has reached such a point today that the very survival of each animal species depends upon its monetary value. If an animal has a high exchange value in monetary terms, it will be ruthlessly hunted for its tusks or its pelt. On the other hand, if it has little or no monetary value, its habitat will be eroded by the more powerful financial forces which demand that habitat for more profitable purposes. The adaptability demanded of the animals today is no longer that of natural selection but financial selection. How are tigers and elephants going to get it right? For human beings, the situation is pretty much the same. As money values increasingly invade traditional economies, the survival of whole peoples depends upon their access to the international money markets, which oppress and sustain them simultaneously.

In late February 1995, the collapse of the Barings Bank sent back shock waves through the stock markets and the banking world. Because of the uncontrolled financial adventures of one man, a twenty-eight-year-old manager of the Singapore branch of the Barings Bank, the entire bank with its four thousand employees and its history of more than two hundred years collapsed. Not only does this telling incident illustrate the uncontrolled development of money and the seamless robe of finance which now girdles the earth, but it reminds us that in all sorts of subtle ways money has become the language of our lives. Money is indeed rather similar to language, as a gigantic creation of human culture which now stands over against human society itself, shaping and modelling that which originally created it. We are now made in the image of what we made.

When Jesus held up a coin and asked whose image and description it had on it, he was suggesting an analogy between human life and coinage. 'Give to Caesar what belongs to Caesar, and to God what belongs to God.' In noticing a similarity between a human personality and a coin, Jesus also established a sharp distinction between them. The human coin, so to speak, is stamped with the likeness of God. Things go wrong when the human personality is stamped with the likeness of the power, authority and other qualities of money itself. This is what is happening in Britain today and throughout all the other money economies. People are being turned into coins. This is a way of saying that the values of human life, including the values of spirituality itself, are taking on the characteristics of money.

This, of course, is concealed from immediate realization. The coin, if we may put it like this, cannot read the image and superscription which is stamped on it. We are unaware of the impact of money upon us. It is in this context that the spiritualities generated by human culture take on such ambiguous and variegated forms.

Spirituality is not the cultivation of the inward

A number of these ambiguous and self-deceptive spiritualities can now be described. First, spirituality is often regarded as the cultivation of the inward. There is a great deal about inner feelings, although it is not clear what outer feelings would be. There is a lot about the inner journey, discovering self-transcendence. This may be described as the introversion of spirituality, and it reflects the money culture in that money tends to atomize communities, to emphasize individuality and to heighten the competitive awareness of one's own interests as opposed to those of other individuals.

Spirituality is not the antithesis of materialism

Another typical tendency of spirituality springing from the money culture is to contrast the spiritual with the material. The spiritual is to be located in the mind, in ideas, in heavenly aspirations and in the so-called spiritual realities. In this way, the spirituality of the money culture distracts attention from its own material base, producing a sort of sublimation of itself. By way of contrast, the true religious spirituality is concerned with the transformation of matter with a genuine materiality. A true spirituality will not seek to become more and more spiritual but will seek to become more and more embodied, more significantly in touch with our bodily existences.

Spirituality is not universal

A third tendency has already been referred to: spirituality is sometimes expressed in terms of universal human nature. People speak about the capacity of human nature to transcend itself through imagination, art and so on. The problem with this approach is that it tends to undervalue the specific historical and social characteristics of the spirituality which is generated in our society by its present human relationships and practices. We make our kind of spirituality universal and timeless, whereas in fact it is specific to each culture. Spirituality is not immutable, not perennial; it is fluid, adaptable, always finding fresh forms.

Spirituality is more than the pursuit of beauty

Finally, there is a tendency to seek the spiritual in the beautiful. It is to be pursued, some say, by cultivating our finer sensitivities, our more insightful perceptions. It is to be located in poetry and music, in the arts and in everything that makes for refinement. Interpreted in this way, spirituality becomes something which families with resources can provide for their children. It becomes a leisure pursuit of the wealthy.

Spirituality as community

If these are examples of the distortions and the deceitful spiritualities produced by the money culture, what is the true spirituality of education? *Spiritual education inspires young people to live for others*. Spirituality exists not inside people but between them. Spirituality seeks to recreate community through participation in the lives of others. This is why in the Christian tradition one speaks of the fellowship of the spirit. The spirit promotes *koinonia* and was understood by St Augustine to be the bond of love which unites the Father and the Son in the Holy Trinity.

Spiritual education is to be distinguished from moral education partly because the latter has to do with notions of right and wrong, and judgements of justice, whereas spirituality is to do with solidarity and communion, and partly because of its inspirational quality. In asking whether the curriculum is making a contribution to the spiritual development of schools and of society, we need to ask of each subject whether it is exploring its potential to inspire young people to live in solidarity with others, rather than offering them a spirituality which will live only too easily with the selfish and individualizing values of the money culture.

Does Religious Education Make Progress?

Winter 1979

We could continue the argument of this article by asking what are the characteristics of religious education during the late eighties and nineties. Perhaps the eighties were marked by progress in phenomenological methods together with an awakening interest in spirituality. The 1990s have been characterized by a blurring of the distinctions between religious education and religious nurture and a sharpening of the boundaries between the religions. They have also been marked by a greater deliberation in seeking to formulate the attainment targets and the assessment procedures used in religious education. It is perhaps too early to make a definite pronouncement on the overall situation, but it seems likely to me that future historians of the subject will reckon that the early eighties represented progress through more careful differentiations, while the late eighties and the nineties represented further progress made, however, against a reactionary backlash.

Can one speak of a religious education in Britain characteristic of the fifties, the sixties, the seventies, and so on? Is it possible to make lists of the emphases of each decade in this way? The sixties, we might say, was the period of experiential Christian education, the seventies the period for world religions, and so on.

If it is possible to describe religious education (or any other social phenomenon) in this way, further interesting questions emerge. What is the relationship between the religious education of one decade and that of the previous decade, and the next? Are we here dealing with a succession of fashions, even of fads, or do we see a process of development, in which each phase is related to the previous and following stages in an evolutionary or organic manner? Moreover, if there is an organic development and not a mere succession of fashions, does it amount to a growth, an improvement in some way, so that we could speak of *progress* in religious education?

Why try to keep abreast of change?

If the relationship between the religious education of the past years and that of the next few years is arbitrary, whimsical, the product of mere fashion, then there is no rational or moral ground for keeping up with it all. If the relationship between one period of religious education and the next *is* rational and a certain teacher or lecturer is up-to-date, but does not really understand the principles of the development, we may describe him or her as being 'trendy'. But if there *are* no principles of development within the subject, then anyone who tries to keep up with it can be nothing but trendy. The cynic observes that if you continue to do and believe just exactly what you do and believe now, you will with the passage of time, once again find yourself in the forefront. This springs from the belief that one stage of religious education passes into the next without principle, and that in effect, we do not learn from the experience of the last decade so as to carry forward with us into the next decade what we have acquired. If that really is our situation, there is no longer much point in trying to think hard and clearly about our work, since we will never be able to improve it. All we can hope to create is yet another random craze, which, like the others, will fade without trace.

Canons of progress?

How would we tell if progress was being made in religious education? If philosophers of science find difficulty in stating the conditions for recognizing progress in science, there need be no embarrassment amongst religious educators about the same question. Let us put the question more carefully. What are the marks which any religious education of the eighties would have to show, in order to defend itself against the charge that it will be nothing but a series of fads and fashions?

We may list four marks of progressive development.

First mark: Differentiation

A subject makes progress if its concepts become increasingly differentiated. First there are only trees. Then there are oaks and cedars. Then there are kinds of cedar. So a botanical taxonomy will be developed, which will be progress, because if there really are so many kinds of trees, the words and descriptions which enable us to speak and think of the differences will bring us that much closer to the real world. This is certainly taking place in religious education. We distinguished in the thirties between preaching and teaching. In the sixties this became a difference between open-ended and closed teaching, and in the early seventies between confessional and professional teaching. Now we distinguish between religious education, religious nurture of faith and religious instruction, and a start is being made in further developing the features of these as being different subjects. Examining this process closely, we see not merely changes in popular vocabulary, but a closer and more discriminating examination of what takes place between teacher and pupil, which brings our thinking closer to reality, and so constitutes progress.

Second mark: Integration

Once features of reality have been noticed, the next step is to bring them together again so as to regard the world as one. Progress is made when the plurality and unity of the world are rediscovered, and seen more tightly and more richly. So within religious education, first we distinguish, as the Schools Council Groundplan did, between religious concepts, feelings and actions. Then we bring all three together, making our presentation of the diverse but unitary religious world that much more realistic. Or we distinguish between several ways of evaluating religion, such as the historical (Did it happen?) the philosophical (Does it make sense?), the ethical (Is it good?) and the psychological (Does it build up personhood?). Then in our teaching we bring these various ways of responding to religion together again.

Third mark: Verification

If the first two marks are present, or seem to be present, in a development of religious education, we must ask if there is any way of verifying the claimed progress towards reality. Here some traces of progress can be seen, but in other areas it is hard to be sure. We distinguished between religions and between cultural groups (mark one) and then, through a theory of pluralism and pluralistic teaching, we advanced to unity (mark two), but can we verify the results? Do we know whether teaching world religions is 'more educational' than teaching the Bible only? Do we know what effect it has upon the faith and religious attitudes of the young when they are placed in pluralistic schools? On the other hand, the Piaget-Goldman psychology enabled us to distinguish certain kinds of thinking about religion (first mark) and the methods of the late sixties (themes, etc.) brought these insights together (second mark). More recent psychological work probably enables us to assess and to diagnose individual learning in religion more realistically. This is surely progress.

Fourth mark: Criticism

In the last resort, a free exchange of rational criticism is the feature of a subject which enables us to distinguish progress from a series of fashions. Are debates in our subject marked by mere assertion, by reiteration of preconceived positions, by use of slogans, by exaggerated claims in which the research evidence is ignored? Then we have fashions. On the other hand, is discussion marked by clarification of ideas, by the encouragement of unusual points of view, in which the evidence is considered and the arguments from previous generations kept in mind? Then there is a sign of progress.

The Religious Education of the Younger Child

Spring 1986

hese reflections occurred to me at a time when Michael Grimmitt, Julie Grove, Louise Spencer and I were beginning the work with young children which was published in 1991 under the title A gift to the child: Religious education in the primary school *(Simon & Schuster/Stanley Thornes). My own reflections about theological conversations with children appeared as* God-talk with young children: Notes for parents and teachers *(Derby, CEM, 1991, and Philadelphia, Trinity Press International, 1991) and* 'Theological conversation with young children' *in* BJRE *(Vol. 20, No. 1).*

In recent years there has been an enormous increase in the number of children under the age of five who are receiving some kind of education. There has not, however, been an upsurge of interest in the religious education of these young children. Indeed, outside the voluntary sector the massive increase in the numbers of nursery-age children has gone almost unnoticed by religious educators.

Two widely held views about the religious education of children seem to have contributed to this strange silence. The first view suggests that it would be educationally unjustifiable to attempt to teach religion to younger children in county schools, because, however attempted, it is bound to nurture religious faith. The second view suggests that younger children cannot understand abstract concepts, and therefore cannot understand religion.

The first view tells us that we *ought* not to do this; the second view tells us that this is something which we *cannot* do successfully. These two views are responsible for the embarrassment and reticence which religious educators have felt when confronted with the vast increase in the numbers of nursery-age children.

Since (as it is often held) younger children cannot understand religious concepts and since (as it is often held) the concepts central to religion are mainly of this kind, the younger children's response to these religious concepts is bound to be of an affective kind. They are bound to respond emotionally, since intellectual response is developmentally beyond them. But (so the thought would run) an affective or emotional response is bound to result in the nurturing of faith, while the cognitive approach is not. One can (it would seem) offer an educationally sound religious education to the more mature children whose cognitive development has reached the stage appropriate to religious concepts, but one cannot do this with younger children. Their immaturity is bound to lead to a response which, being mainly emotional, will nurture them in faith in a manner which will be educationally improper in the county school. It is time, however, that these views were challenged.

Concepts or conversation?

The meanings and the emotions of words are always encountered in sentences and not in mere vocabulary. The words in a dictionary are not found in such a form in ordinary speech, where they are always in discourse or in talk, not arranged in alphabetical order. Young children do not merely encounter concepts, they participate in conversation. Whether children will inevitably be nurtured in religious faith, or (even worse) indoctrinated, depends not upon the inevitable emotional association of concepts, or the disorganized emotional rubble which accumulates (as it seems to be suggested) when the concept cannot be comprehended, but upon the flexibility and the range of meanings represented in actual conversation.

The dominance of cognitive psychology

It is because discussion of the problem of the religious education of younger children has centred upon the philosophy of concepts, as mediated by cognitive developmental psychology, that the two views which we are questioning have arisen. Concepts are sometimes spoken of as if they subsisted within some kind of inner space (the mind?) and cognitive development is sometimes spoken of as if it took place in isolation from its social context. Belief in the isolation of the maturing mind is joined with belief in the isolation of concepts and rests upon belief in the isolation of words. These tendencies when applied to the study of the religious education of young children must be questioned in the name of conversation. Conversation is inter-personal, it is relational, social and communal. In order to understand conversation we need to call upon the resources offered by discourse analysis, hermeneutics, psycho-social theories of the self, and socialization theory. A religious education theory for young children enriched by such disciplines might look rather different from the somewhat arid, individualistic and purely conceptual approach of the older analytic educational philosophy.

Adult verbalisms

There is no reason why we should expect that young children will naturally think of God as an old man in the sky. No doubt their thinking about God will be pre-concrete operational, and we should never forget how varied and surprising such thought can be, but the particular image of the old man in the sky is the product of socialization. The structural demands of developmental stages do not impose upon children's speech and imagination any particular content. The content is drawn from conversation. It is from detheologized adults that young children pick up such clichés (these are little more than verbalisms): God is male, is old, looks after us, makes flowers grow, and that we go to be with Jesus when we die, etc. What we find in this repertoire of childlike religiosity is very little intrinsic to childhood but a great deal which indicates the puerilization of adult religious life.

Perhaps we have been too ready to apply the words 'concrete' or 'pre-concrete' to conversations about God with young children. When God is imagined he is by definition imaged, but although the images of God which children employ often have features which reflect the immediate experience of the children, there is little reason to believe that *as images* they are more concrete than the images of God used by adults. Moreover, there seems little reason to believe that the thinking of young children about God must be confined to images. Young children are also capable of forming concepts, and although these will be relatively crude compared with those of thoughtful adults, they may well contain elements of generalization and thus of abstraction. In this way such concepts will differ from images, which are necessarily specific and pictorial.

It is possible by the deliberate introduction of conflicting or alternative images to encourage young children to generalize about these images and thus to begin the process of conceptualization. Thus, if young children ask whether God is very old, they could be told that God is very young, like a baby. If they ask whether God is a man, they could be told that God is like a woman. If they ask whether God is very big, one answer could be that God is very small. Concepts may conflict, but images enrich the imagination when they are multiplied.

God-talk with children

While it is no doubt quite true that young children should appreciate that God is to be spoken of with reverence (and it can be assumed that atheist teachers will speak of God with the same reverence, since not to speak of God reverently would be to give children a false impression of how religious conversation about God is conducted), conversations about God should also take place in a quizzical and often humorous spirit. The important thing is to explore different styles of conversation, rather than to transmit any particular concept. Young children can be introduced to the gods of Greece, of the Nordic myths and of modern world faiths. If young children ask how many gods there are, an adult may reply that perhaps there are millions and millions, but some people say that there is one and some people say there is none.

The important thing is to introduce the vocabulary conversationally and so widen the repertoire of the children. Experience suggests that far from confusing children, this approach encourages delight, play and curiosity.

Conversational techniques with young children may be based upon the traditional ways of speaking about the divine. So we may use the negative method (God is not a horse, not a man or woman, not a baby, not big, not little), the positive method (God is king, father, mother, child), the way of analogy (God is *like* a father, *like* a mother), the dialectical method (he is like a baby because he is new and fresh but he is not like a baby because he will always be new and fresh), the way of experience (I felt that God was near me) and the way of story (once, when God made the world ...).

Through such conversational techniques, younger children can be effectively socialized into God-talk, and they can also develop an enjoyment and a curiosity regarding religious language. They can be set free from fixation on a particular image or concept which might later restrict more systematic understandings.

Would it be possible to train adults, whether parents, nursery nurses or teachers, in such conversation arts? Would it be possible for such adults to learn how to converse with young children so that their intelligence about religion would be increased? Could this be done in a multi-cultural context, and be of value to all children whether they have a religious or a secular background?

Religious Education in the Primary School

November 1971

Since the mid-1960s there have been three main waves of new religious education agreed syllabuses in England and Wales. In the late 1960s, the new syllabuses concentrated upon child-centred and experiential approaches, while those of the later 1970s and the early 1980s emphasized the teaching of world religions. The leading new syllabuses of the 1990s combine the interest in world religions with the experiential approach, offering teachers a wide range of possible schemes of work. This extract is a comment upon the first of these waves. No attempt has been made to relate it to more recent developments. However, it does help us to understand the significance of the syllabuses of today.

Religious education in the primary school has in recent years been passing through a period of rapid development. The work of psychologists such as R.S. Lee, Violet Madge, Eve Lewis and above all, Ronald Goldman, created a new interest in the limits and possibilities of children's understanding of religion and led to extensive revision of syllabuses. On the whole, direct use of the Bible with stories of Christian heroes gave way to a content more appropriate to child-centred education and to methods such as experiential religious education and life themes. During the same period, religious education was deeply influenced by changes, such as the integrated day, taking place in the general primary curriculum.

Many teachers of young children have now adopted these changes with insight and enthusiasm. Others are still confused and uncertain. Realizing that it is now no longer considered adequate simply to retell Bible stories but not seeing exactly what else to do, some teachers have given up the struggle and in a few primary schools religious education is in danger of disappearing. Misunderstanding created suspicion of the new methods which were sometimes wrongly thought to spring from a desire to eliminate the Bible from the primary school.

Various other factors have contributed to the crisis. While some colleges of education have been active in pioneering the new approaches others have either neglected courses on methods or have continued to teach methods which are no longer relevant to the situation that the young teacher will meet in the schools. The extensive in-service retraining which the rapid changes call for has not been carried out as thoroughly as might have been expected. The growing numbers of children belonging to various religious communities present the teacher with a new set of perplexities. Oddly enough little research has been done to complement that of Goldman, and, as a result, the new syllabuses are built upon a foundation of scientific knowledge insufficiently wide to support them. Worst of all perhaps, methods such as teaching through life themes have been accepted without being subjected to enough critical appraisal of their objectives and inner logic.

The result in late 1971 is a scene of astonishing diversity. Will the crises be successfully resolved? Because of the high quality of work being done by a few teachers there is reason to hope so. Reports from various parts of the country indicate that teachers are finding that the problems can be dealt with and that religious education can become an exciting part of the young child's school experience.

Teaching Religion through Artefacts

Summer and Autumn 1986

Part I

The use of artefacts is one of the most rapidly growing methods for the teaching of religion in British classrooms. Many shops specializing in Asian goods have religious education teachers amongst their best customers. It is increasingly common to find that religious education in-service courses will have not only a bookstall but an artefact shop, and in teachers' centres and religious education groups up and down the country one finds people busily engaged in the collection and annotation of boxes of artefacts.

Although a number of well-informed and energetic religious educators are contributing very effectively to the classroom teacher's awareness of the possibilities of artefacts, and the actual range of such objects currently being used in the classroom seems to be expanding almost week by week, not so much has been done to deepen understanding of the nature of the method itself. This is perfectly in order, since in the resourcing of classroom teaching, as in cooking, the principle must often be 'first catch your chicken'. There is a place, however, to ask ourselves what artefacts are, and how we should use them.

Artefacts and resources

The difference between an artefact and a resource is simple enough. An artefact is an object which has its natural location in the life of the religious community which it typifies. A resource, however, is made in order to serve the needs of education. Thus a domestic shrine statue of Lord Krishna is an artefact. It is something which one would find naturally situated in the home of a devotee. A set of slides on devotion to Krishna together with a cassette produced for use in religious education classes would, however, be a resource. A set of coloured pictures for classroom display illustrating the five Ks of the Sikh tradition would be a resource, but of the actual objects four would be artefacts (the comb, the shorts, the small curved sword and the metal bangle) while the final K would be a natural object (the uncut hair). It is true, of course, that when artefacts are used in the classroom they may be thought of as a kind of resource. The point is, however, that in order to use them properly we must pay attention to *what* kind of resources they are.

Artefacts are made by people

As the cognate word 'artificial' reminds us, an artefact is a human-made object. Thus, while a religious artefact is an object which has its natural habitat in the religious community which uses it, not all such objects are artefacts. A conch shell, although an object which is used regularly in Hindu worship, is not an artefact because it is not made by human hands. The same would be true of flowers used in worship, and of the human hair, whether cut off, as in the case of Christian nuns, or uncut, as in the case of Sikhs. If a meteorite or natural, uncarved stone should be used in worship by a religious group, it would not be thought of as an artefact unless it had been subject to carving and shaping by human workers.

Artefacts are small

Temples and pyramids, aqueducts and highways, huge carvings on cliff-faces and megalithic stone monuments would not usually be described as artefacts. We can thus distinguish the artefacts of a religion from its architecture. In religious education we usually describe as artefacts those religious objects which we bring into the classroom. Classroom artefacts need to be supplemented by field visits. When pupils visit a temple or a church, they can discover not only the religious architecture and the interior furnishings, but also see some artefacts like statues which would be too large or too inconvenient to bring into the classroom.

Artefacts are three-dimensional

It is customary to distinguish between the art and the artefacts of a culture. Murals and wall-paintings, friezes and icons are not normally considered to be artefacts. It is also customary to distinguish the artefacts of a culture from its inscriptions. One would not usually describe books or parchments, monuments or inscribed obelisks as artefacts.

There are, of course, many intermediate cases. Artefacts such as jewellery or medallions may carry inscriptions, and illustrations may be painted upon the surface of vases. Our discussion, however, leads us to a definition of artefacts which will be clear enough for our educational purposes: an artefact is a small (let us say, smaller than the human body), three-dimensional product of human culture.

What artefacts would you take with you if you were banished to a desert island? Which artefacts from your home would you take if you were going on a mission to another planet in order to show them what we human beings are like? Of all the artefacts in your own house, which do you value most and why? Have you ever made an artefact?

Religious artefacts

Religious artefacts are simply those which are used for religious purposes or which are characteristically found in religious contexts. These might include the communion chalice in Christianity, a domestic shrine dedicated to Siva in

Hinduism, or a Jewish *seder* plate. Of course when the object is brought into the classroom, it is no longer under religious usage, nor is it located in its religious context; instead of *actual* use, we must now speak of *intended* use. A religious artefact is a way of studying religious intentions. Religious intentions include not only the intention to do something (e.g. the intention to celebrate a ritual) but also the intention to be reminded of something or to feel something (a cross worn as a necklace), to cause something to happen (e.g. by the ringing of a bell) and so on. Religious artefacts thus open the door to religious meanings of many kinds.

The study of religious meanings through artefacts

If through religious artefacts we are introducing our pupils to religious meanings, then we are asking our pupils to interpret. The art of interpretation is involved every time an artefact is used in religious education. To do this most effectively, we need to consider what it is like to interpret a religious meaning, and what the characteristics of such religious interpretations are.

The most immediate way of interpreting a religious meaning is by face-to-face dialogue in conversation with a religious believer. The believer is the first witness of faith, and since all religious meanings are human meanings, it is the humans who intend those meanings who are the unique and irreplaceable sources for entering into and appreciating the nature of religious faith and commitment. This is why no matter how popular and widespread the use of artefacts might become, conversation both between pupils and religious believers and between teachers and pupils about religion will continue to be the chief method for the teaching of religion.

If this first, most immediate, form of interpreting religious meanings is not possible, because religious people are not available for such conversation, or if, in any case, it is desirable to change the method away from conversation itself, the next most effective way of approaching religious meanings would be through inscription of one kind or another. The spoken word is the first carrier of religious meaning. The written word is the second. The written or inscribed word may be in the form of books, sacred texts, letters and diaries, or handwritten notes. The inscribed word may also take the form of magnetic tape, cassette or video, gramophone record or compact disc.

The inscribed word places the meaning at one distance removed. The speakers or writer cannot now be questioned immediately as to their meaning. Questions arise about the circumstances in which he or she wrote, and the original audience to whom the communication was addressed, to say nothing of changes in meaning which may have occurred in the language itself, especially if the inscription is old. If even the written form of speech is unavailable, then we must turn to objects. Because these are objects intentionally made by human beings, they enshrine human intentions. Without words, however, the artefact is like a code. Its silence is enigmatic. The artefact will need words to unlock it. Most artefacts will have a story to accompany them, and the combination of story and thing will bring out the religious meaning.

Beyond the artefact lies the fourth and most remote way of discovering religious meaning. We come to the natural object – the stone, the lump of uncarved wood, the meteorite, the plant or animal. Here we encounter objects which are not the product of human intentions, and do not provide easy clues to human meanings. Nevertheless, such natural objects may become the carriers of many human meanings and may be caught up in a web of revelation and interpretation, as occurs, for example, with the conch shell in Hinduism or the ram's horn in Judaism.

Close and distant meanings

Only when we place the religious artefact in this hierarchy of meanings can we gain a clear idea of the particular problems and the fascinating possibilities which are offered to the religious educator by these objects. Although the artefact is, as we have shown, the most removed of the various ways by which we can understand human meanings, it is equally true that the very concrete and tangible nature of the artefact gives the religious meaning, in spite of its enigmatic qualities, a vividness and a powerful presence which may have a profound effect upon young people and children, if presented in the right way. We remind ourselves now that the artefact is not an illustration, it is not a model, it is not a mere attention-catcher. It is an actual embodiment in three dimensions of a human religious meaning. It is a living part of the actual world of religion, a fragment of the phenomenon of religious experience, transported into the classroom and available for story, for meditation and for discussion. In the artefact we reach a kind of religious education which is a 'hands-on' activity.

How to use artefacts

The clue to the use of the artefact in the classroom lies in the strange combination of hidden and often rather general meaning which is silently present in the artefact, and (on the other hand) the specific and concrete nature of this actual object as it is held in the hand. We may think of a coin as being a typical artefact. This coin which I hold in my hand is smooth and worn with the rubbings of many pockets, many purses, many fingers and thumbs. Who knows where it has been and what it has done? There are many others like it, and it represents something of great abstraction in our currency and in our economic life. Yet it remains *this* coin. I feel its hard edges. I bite it. I read its inscriptions. I feel its weight in the lining of my coat. It is concrete and general at the same time.

The approach to the general is through the concrete. This means that when we are teaching artefacts we first must approach this particular artefact in all of its uniqueness and its actuality. We must be in its presence, open to its voice, in tune with its peculiarities. The artefact must be examined, possibly handled, moved around, looked at in different lights, and in every way we must make the artefact a familiar object to our senses. Gradually, through questioning, the inner meaning of the artefact will disclose itself. That particular aspect of the religious world to which the particular artefact belongs will be disclosed by story and by song. Step by step, the wealth of emotion which hangs around that object will be extended first to the category of objects and then to an understanding of the commitment and worship of believers who go beyond that object into the presence of the holy.

Can we do this in the classroom? The artefact is essentially an aid to an encounter. If we can create in our classrooms places for religious encounter, then we can find in our classrooms a contemporary use for the religious artefact.

Part II
Teaching from artefacts

A religious artefact, as we have seen, is a small three-dimensional object made by people to express a religious intention or to fulfill a religious function, and which has its natural habitat in the religious life of the individual or the community. One possible method for teaching religion through such artefacts is based upon the idea that the artefact is essentially ambiguous, more ambiguous than inscribed language, and very much more ambiguous that the actual presence of the religious people who made or use the artefact and who can actually tell you face to face what they meant by it. It is because artefacts are both concrete and ambiguous that this kind of method is suggested, and this is also related to the distinction between the close meaning and the distant meaning of the artefact. The close meaning is what the artefact immediately tells you upon inspection; the distant meaning is the belief-world out of which it comes, and the actions, hopes and intentions which are or were once expressed through this object. The distant meaning might include the mythology, the theology, the festival or ritual in which this object once played a part, or which it represented in some way.

The gulf between the close meaning and the distant meaning

What one finds so often in teaching from artefacts is that there is a gulf between the close meaning and the distant meaning. What the object yields to immediate examination by children in class is often far removed from the cultural and the religious context which the thing has when placed or used in its natural religious world. It is all very well to insist that the artefact must be allowed to speak for itself, but what it will say to pupils in one context will be different from what it will say to them in another context, what it will say in the West may be quite different from what it will say in the East. The problem lies precisely in the fact that the artefact does not *say* anything; rather it is we who interpret its meaning, or what we imagine its meaning to be.

Let us take two examples from Sikhism. When the sacred book (*Guru Granth Sahib*) is being read, it is normal to rest it upon a cushion, to drape it with cloths and to place it under a decorative canopy. The reader will hold a ceremonial sceptre or mace in the form of a whisk in his or her right hand and this will be waved over the book to indicate its authority. In these various ways the worshippers in the gurdwara express the honour and devotion which they feel not only towards the book but towards the living tradition of the gurus themselves.

Let us suppose that in a collection of Sikh artefacts for classroom use, the cushion, the cloths and the ceremonial whisk (*chauri*) were included. What would the close meaning, the initial impact, of these items be upon a class of British schoolchildren? The trouble is that the cushion is so ordinary that it is misleading, while the *chauri* is so unusual that it is equally misleading. The teacher could ask a class of junior children whether, if a very important visitor came to the house, the family would seat the visitor on a plain, wooden, kitchen chair. From here, it might be possible to go on to the idea of a throne, adorned with robes and cushions. There is, however, little that can be gained from a mere examination of the cushion itself, whereas when the artefact happens to be (let us say) a wall hanging depicting the Golden Temple, discussion quickly leads to something which is of religious importance. There is the added problem that the chair as an article of furniture has a very different place in oriental domestic life. Perhaps the way into this artefact would not be through the place of the chair at all, but through considering pictures and stories in which something precious is placed on a cushion – for example, a royal crown or a golden slipper. Whatever the approach, it remains the case that as a religious artefact a cushion is both too familiar and too vague.

The case of the *chauri* lies at the opposite pole of a similar difficulty. If the cushion is familiar and rather commonplace, the *chauri* is a striking object, a rather peculiar object, something almost entirely unfamiliar, and something about which all kinds of comical and bizarre suggestions are likely to be made by lively youngsters. Many children will say that the *chauri* reminds them of the Olympic torch. One can see why. The long shiny, metal rod is obviously some kind of handle, and the instinct is to hold it upright, rather than point it down, and to pretend that the flame-shaped tuft of long, tapering hair is like a torch, or like candy floss or Mr Whippy's soft ice-cream cone. It is not advisable to start waving a *chauri* in front of a high-spirited class of twelve-year-olds, asking, 'What would you use this for?' In the case of the cushion the question seems daft. In the case of the *chauri* the question seems provocative. If the cushion is so ordinary that it says little, the *chauri* is so unusual that it says lots of different things. Should we simply not try to use them as religious artefacts?

Finding bridges between close and distant meanings

When the close meaning of an artefact offers no easy access to its distant meaning, bridges must be built. A poem, a story, a song or a picture may be such bridges. If the bridge can be another artefact, so much the better. Often artefacts are best presented in associated groups, each one being used to interpret the others in its group. Let us suppose that we have a picture which shows a Sikh reading the sacred book, the latter being placed under the canopy on the cushion and with the *chauri* waved above it. Let us suppose that the picture is not a Western artist's impression or an illustration from a textbook, but a print such as might be found in the home of a Sikh, or may be a scene depicted on a medallion, a car-sticker or some other object which is a natural part of present-day Sikh life in Britain. The picture provides the commentary upon the objects. 'Can you see an object like this in this picture? What makes you think that the book from which this distinguished-looking gentleman is reading is a very special book? In what ways does a Sikh show that *Guru Granth Sahib* has authority? What are the signs or symbols of authority in your school or your home?'

Four steps in method

This discussion enables us to distinguish four stages in the presentation of an artefact in a religious education lesson. First, there is the investigative or interrogative stage. This is the stage when the object makes its own initial impact upon the children. They are invited to hold it, to feel its weight, to notice this and that about it, to make suggestions about its nature and its use. It is at this preliminary stage that the close meanings will be presented. Sometimes the religious meaning of the object will be obvious but sometimes it will not.

Secondly, there comes the bridging stage. Now the close meaning is interpreted and clarified through a story or a picture, and so on. This second step is particularly important when the artefact is rather unexciting, or (on the other hand) when it is alien from the children's experience, or when it is simply totally mystifying.

Thirdly, there is the 'announcement' stage or the 'systems' stage. Here the teacher gives information about the religious context of the object, places the object within the systematic structure of the religion, encourages the pupil to find out facts about the living context of the thing. The pupils learn something of the origins and history of *Guru Granth Sahib,* come to know that every copy of the book is exactly the same in its layout, and learn more about the way in which the book is reverenced by Sikhs.

Finally, we have what might be called the stage of 'application' or 'extension'. This is the point where the religious education teacher invites his or her pupils not only to learn about the object but to learn from the object. What is there about this artefact and its place in religious life which has something to offer to these young people which will be of relevance in their own personal and social lives? We have now studied the artefact, but what can it teach us about ourselves? What is its message to us? We have evaluated it; now it asks questions of us. What authorities do we acknowledge? How does our society symbolize its authority structure? Is it right that anybody or anything should have authority over us, or should we not rather all be equals? Now, phenomenology has passed through religious studies into experiential education.

Summary

In the teaching of artefacts we pass through four stages: asking, contextualizing, telling and applying. The wheel has come full circle. We began by bringing our ordinary experiences to this object in our questioning of it; now we come back to the ordinary experiences which we have had. Life interprets religion, and religion interprets life. Minds are opened, not closed. Options are widened, not narrowed. Teachers and pupils are left with more questions, not more answers.

Religious Education through Story

Summer 1982

Story-telling, one of the oldest arts of the religious educator, is being reborn. Several factors seem to be at work here. Sociologists and psychologists have emphasized the role of story in establishing personal identity and cultural continuity. An interesting genre of contemporary theology seeks to use the basic categories of story to interpret the significance of Christian faith, while an increased familiarity with world religions is opening up for teachers rich resources of stories from Islam, Buddhism, Hinduism, Judaism and other religions. In British religious education we may also note that many teachers are turning to the arts in an attempt to find ways of creating an understanding of religion which will go beyond the merely factual and which will enable children and young people to respond to the religious vision with the heart as well as with the mind, without departing from strictly educational aims and objectives.

The story and the catechism may be thought of as representing the two oldest and most representative methods in religious education. If we may look upon the catechism as representing the doctrinal, the intellectual, the question-and-answer method which seeks both to transmit received teachings and to promote critical understanding, we may look upon the story as representing the imaginative, the dramatic, that which challenges one to personal discovery and to ethical decision, as that method which seeks to express the spirit and the inner values of a religion. There will always be a certain tension between the catechetical type of religious education and the story type.

There is no doubt that the Goldman approach with its interest in life themes and its tendency to emphasize implicit religious education, led to a hesitation on the part of many teachers in using stories. In so far as this represented an abrupt challenge to the naive and often literalistic use of the Bible story in religious education, it was a helpful and necessary movement. What we need is the critique of the story method in religious education not from the *outside* (by the catechetical type of alternative) but from *within*. The story method itself needs to be expanded so as to rid it of its naive literalism. It needs to be placed within an educational theory embracing both the teaching of world religions and an interest in the personal development of the pupil. An adequate theory of the story in an educational context demands a contemporary knowledge of the place of religion itself in healthy and normal child development. Sometimes the reassertion of the story method takes the form of a suspicious rejection of the catechetical method. However, these two traditional methods of religious education need each other, supplement each other and correct each other. The recent discoveries of the critical, rational, intellectualism of children's religious life must be *taken up into* a renewed understanding of the educational significance of religious stories. The rebirth of the story method must not be looked upon as a correction of a distortion or the *adding* of what had been omitted or overlooked in the other emphasis.

One of the striking features of the story method is that it is equally applicable to all age groups. Socrates used the catechetical method when he wanted to expose the ignorance of his pupils, but when he wanted to reveal the inner heart of his positive teaching, he used stories. But the stories of both Socrates and Jesus were addressed to adults not to children. There is nothing about the story which is particularly appropriate for children, and it would be wrong to think of the story as if its proper place was in the infant and junior school. It does, of course, have a vital role to play with the young child, but it is important that secondary teachers should feel comfortable in the telling of stories and that the assumptions which adolescent pupils bring to their religious education lessons will not be such that stories will be thought of as infantile.

Teaching the Bible
Summer and Autumn 1983

This item was expanded to become 'The Bible in the Secular Classroom' most recently reprinted in J. Astley and D.V. Day (eds), The Contours of Christian Education (McCrimmon, 1992, pp. 107–215).

Learning about the Bible

Much religious education is intended to help pupils learn *about* the Bible. Some of this material could be called 'background to the Bible' and consists of information about the daily life and customs of the people in the Bible. We may also include under this heading lesson material which considers the external history of the Bible – the history of its text, translations, influence and spread throughout the world. A third type of 'teaching about the Bible' is the study of the influence of the Bible upon literature or music or art.

The reasons why 'learning about the Bible' has been so popular are clear enough. Teaching of this kind avoids controversial religious questions, can be thought of as being academic in an objective, factual sense, especially if some ancillary study such as archaeology is included, and does something to establish the cultural relevance of the Bible. It should also be said that the material is not without interest to many teachers and young people.

The weaknesses of 'learning about the Bible' are also evident. Just because such teaching avoids dealing with the central messages of the Bible, it may be questioned whether it should really be regarded as religious education at all. In this approach, the Bible is treated as an historical book, a cultural book, an exciting book, and possibly as a moral book, but not as a religious book.

Learning the Bible

There is another way of teaching the Bible in British schools. Far from being indirect, or dealing with the Bible from an external point of view, this approach introduces the pupil immediately to the text of the Bible. Indeed, in some of its forms, this way of teaching the Bible involves nothing but the text of the Bible. In the controversies of the nineteenth century, many nonconformists did not want the Bible taught in the schools at all, because they thought that the church was the place for such teaching, but if the Bible was to be taught in schools, then it should be without note or comment. The reason for this was the fear that the teachers might give a denominational interpretation of the Bible if they were allowed to make any comment on it. One can see from this that such an approach did have a certain externality in that no attempt could be made to relate the Bible to the lives of pupils, and the text stood alone, without being mediated by the experiences of teacher or pupil.

The so-called 'simple Bible teaching' of the late nineteenth and early twentieth centuries was a development of this approach. Now, indeed, the basic doctrines of the Bible were taught. This, at least, was what the advocates of 'simple Bible teaching' believed but it was often pointed out that the result was to teach Christianity as interpreted by evangelical Protestantism.

From those early beginnings, the movement to 'learn the Bible' gathered impetus, and from the period well before the First World War right up until the 1950s, progressive religious education in this country was mainly preoccupied with the problems of communicating to the young a worthwhile understanding of the biblical documents interpreted in the light of scholarship. The movement gained force during the period between the wars, sometimes under the impact of neo-orthodoxy, and was further strengthened by the 'biblical theology' movement in the 1940s and 1950s. Although there was considerable interest throughout the whole of this fifty-year period in the psychological problems of relating material appropriately to the age and the development of the pupil, and a similar interest in the pedagogical problems of communicating a lively understanding and a sense of involvement with the biblical text, it remained true that the Bible itself was always the major focus of interest. It was largely taken for granted that a knowledge and an understanding of the Bible would contribute to the personal development of pupils, and it was also taken for granted that the direction of this development would be towards a Christian discipleship. The Bible continued to function as 'the Word of God' in a way which was only implicit in the 'learning about the Bible' approach. When one 'learnt the Bible' in the sense we are now discussing, such a teaching and learning was from faith to faith. This comment is, of course, not made in criticism of that approach in its own day, but in order to clarify the situation of the Bible in British religious education today.

Learning from the Bible

Two major factors affect the place of the Bible in contemporary religious education. The first of these may be expressed by saying that the Bible can no longer address the pupil 'from faith'. The Bible will be taught by a teacher in whose religious education syllabus a variety of sacred literature will appear. Other sacred scriptures can no longer be relegated to a sixth-form course on 'non-Christian religions'. Although the Bible retains some cultural and religious relevance in British schools, its position is affected by the fact that in principle it must now be considered as a member of a class, namely, one sacred book amongst others.

The second factor is that the teaching of the Bible can no longer be 'to faith'. It would no longer be right to assume, let alone to intend, that the teaching of the Bible should promote Jewish faith or Christian discipleship. The contribution of the Bible towards the religious educational process must be construed differently. It is at this point that we must speak of 'learning *from* the Bible'.

To learn *from* the Bible naturally includes both learning *about* the Bible and learning the Bible, but the focus is different, and that means that often the selection of material and the classroom methods will also be different. Here, we are mainly concerned with the personal development of our students. They are to learn as persons, to deepen their humanity through learning, to learn their way into values, commitments, beliefs and aspirations, and this learning is to be carried on in dialogue with the Bible. This learning is to be stimulated by the Bible; the Bible is to be the agent of this learning. It is primarily themselves that pupils are learning about, and the Bible is that book which tells them about themselves. They may, or may not, come to accept that view of themselves which is presented in the Bible, because the Bible will not be presented as being normative or as having any intrinsic right to prescribe what they shall be, or as possessing any authority to declare the truth, for this authority is accessible only to faith.

It is at this point that 'learning from the Bible' in our secular, educational, multi-faith classrooms will differ from Christian experiential Bible teaching. In that approach, passages from the Bible were laid alongside aspects of the lives of young people so that a sort of mutual illumination or convergence took place, the Bible being presented as the normative interpreter of life experiences, in the hope that students would share the biblical point of view. 'Learning from the Bible' does not make these assumptions. *What* pupils conclude about themselves is something that goes beyond the scope of education, but it is the duty of the educator to ensure that the *process* of self-discovery shall take place in contact with the arts and the sciences and so on, and in the case of the religious educator this means that the self-discovery of the pupil must proceed by way of the sacred literature and the religious communities and, in particular, the Bible.

Learning from the Bible, understood in this way, is faithful to the requirements of education, since it does not propose to control learning but only to promote it. This approach is also faithful to the nature and meaning of the Bible itself, because the Bible is the story of how generation after generation of people learned how to learn. In learning from the Bible our pupils may become continuous with the people of the Bible, entering into that world of wonder and mystery and discovery, not in the sense that they will become members of the community of faith, but in the sense that they will be confronted with the question of faithfulness and destiny, responsibility and community, identity and service, questions which continually challenged the people of the Bible. Central to the conception of the place of the Bible in modern religious education is the idea that the Bible is not to be considered as a human book about God, but rather God's book about people. It is not so much a book in which religious answers are offered to the human questions of life, God being thought of as one such 'answer', but it is a book which presents itself as a record of revelation, a story of God's dealing with the human race, and thus a record of God's concern for people and of the nature and meaning of human life within the creation and the covenant of God. This understanding of the Bible is not only phenomenologically adequate, in that this is indeed how the Bible appears to the student of religion, but it is also adequate to faith, since that is how faith appears to itself and how it receives the Bible. It is also adequate to the needs of education, since it provides a rationale for human development in relation to this particular sacred record of the education of humanity.

The teaching of the Bible in the county schools today cannot be 'from faith to faith'. Faith has always been the context within which the Bible has been interpreted, preached and taught. If today we are to discover a rationale for the teaching of the Bible in an educational way, a way which does not exclude faith but does not require faith or assume faith, it means looking at the Bible in a very different way.

Two views of the Bible

Visitors to Coventry Cathedral will be familiar with the famous transformation in perspective which takes place when the visitor, having walked down the nave, reaches the altar and turning around, looks back down the nave towards the west door. The view from the footpath, through the glass doors of the western entrance, shows a cathedral full of rich and interesting detail. The green, brown and grey of the interior lead the observer past the 'Words of Witness' on both sides of the nave, until one is standing before the huge tapestry of Christ in glory. Turning around, the view from the alter reveals a cathedral transformed by the light of the panels of stained glass, previously invisible. From the altar, the 'Words of Witness' can no longer be seen, and as one gazes out from the heart of the cathedral towards the city everything is radiant.

So it is with the Bible. There is a view of the Bible 'from the street'. From this perspective, the Bible is full of colourful and interesting scenes, and as one is led on, one is challenged by the questions about life and destiny which are thrown by the Bible at its readers. All of this is available from the secular viewpoint. There is another view of the Bible which is available only to the believer, the one who stands in the heart of the Bible looking out at the world with the vision of faith. The Bible is then transformed with light.

It may well be that the secular and the religious ways of understanding the Bible need each other. They complement each other. But it would be wrong to insist that one view had nothing worthwhile to offer without the other. The religious view of the Bible has brought radiant meaning into the lives of millions of believers who were so nurtured within the bosom of the church and in biblical faith that they never experienced any other way of understanding the Bible. Similarly, the Bible may enrich the knowledge and insight of many a secular person who examines the Bible from a secular point of view, even though he or she may not come to share in the faith of the Bible.

A book for all humanity

Surely the Bible is not only a book for a few religious traditions. It is also a book which deals with certain fundamental human themes. Anybody who has experienced loss, or who has exercised power and been subjected to power, anyone who has gazed in amazement at nature or who has pondered on the destiny of a nation, anyone who has known great human love or who has suffered from terrible human frailty will be able to find in the Bible a literature which springs from experiences such as these and points beyond them. It is through the exploration of such common human themes that the Bible may often be best taught today.

But the Bible is claimed by Jews and Christians as if it were their private property. The Church, it is often said, came before the Bible and is the only legitimate interpreter of the Bible. Thus, it is often said, the Bible can be understood only in the light of Christian doctrine, or in the context of the Church's traditions.

Such claims, must, however, be rejected. The Bible is not the book of the Church; it is the book of the Kingdom of God. Just as it is increasingly recognized today that we cannot identify the Church with the Kingdom but must regard the Church as a witness to the Kingdom, so the Bible also must be seen as the book which points to the Kingdom.

The Bible is like a vast, ancient and beautiful palace of mirrors in which one particular tribe has squatted. The squatters now claim to own the palace because their ancestors built it, and they deny access to anyone who is not a member of their tribe. The protest against this tribalization of the Bible should be modelled upon the protest of Jesus against the tribalization of the Temple when he said, 'My house shall be called a house of prayer for all nations.'

**Principles for the
interpretation of the Bible**

So we see that while faith, religion and the Church are legitimate principles for the interpretation of the Bible, they are to be supplemented by lack of faith, secularity, and ecumenicity in the broadest sense. The Bible is not only a religious book; it is a secular book. It is true that it can be interpreted in the light of faith but it is not true that it *must* be interpreted in the light of faith. That which is merely human may also offer guidelines for the interpretation of the Bible. This is to say that our common humanity, whether in faith or not, whether in the Church or not, offers us certain principles from which the Bible may be understood and to which the Bible may direct its questions.

If this is so, then we have discovered an educational way of proceeding in the secular classrooms of today. That way is to enable pupils to learn from the Bible. Pupils, in learning from the Bible, are learning about themselves, or meeting with various questions which will challenge any conception they may have of themselves. This view of the Bible is a view 'from the street', that is, a view from the perspective provided by our common humanity. It may be complemented by a teaching *about* the Bible in which it will be shown that the Bible is not only a book for all humanity but is in a special way a book which exercises a tremendous influence within certain religious groups. The existential and the phenomenological may thus be linked. This way of teaching the Bible will be educationally acceptable because the Bible will stimulate learning and will not seek to direct or control the outcome of that learning. Moreover, since the idea that the Bible throws doubts upon our assumptions about the nature of our humanity arises when the Bible is thought of as God's quest for people, this view of the Bible and of how to teach it would be rather different from the liberal, critical view of the Bible as a *human* book about God which dominated religious education in this country for the first fifty years of the twentieth century. In response to the question 'What is humanity?' the Bible replies that humanity is that which is lost, searched for and found by God. The pupil who approaches the Bible through religious education today will not necessarily come to share the biblical view of humanity nor even necessarily come to accept that it can correctly be described as God's anthropology. But he or she must at least entertain the possibility and this possibility is sufficient to make the Bible a resource book for human learning.

Religious Education through Fantasy

Autumn 1987

Religion has seldom felt comfortable with fantasy. Father Christmas, we are sometimes told, should not be associated with God or even with Jesus for when children learn the truth about the reindeers and the delightfully full stockings they will also give up belief in God. Having been taken in by one pretty fantasy, they are unlikely to be deceived a second time. Similar fears are often expressed about associating fairy stories with stories from the Bible and other religious traditions.

Why this fear of the fabulous? This may be looked upon as a by-product of the impact of the eighteenth-century Enlightenment upon religion. The rise of biblical criticism destroyed the idea that the Bible was a simple record of fact, and in reaction there was a tendency on the part of some believers to assert the truth of the simple facts, even claiming as facts what in earlier centuries had been interpreted spiritually or allegorically. Precisely because of the threat to it, the Bible now bristled with facts, and a religious faith which did not know which way it would go if the whole notion of fact were undermined increasingly disassociated itself from fantasy.

An outstanding example of this reaction can be found in the famous series of films produced from within American conservative Christianity from the 1950s onwards called 'Fact and Faith'. Faith was based on facts. The facts of faith were as factual as those of science – indeed, they were the facts of science. Scientific fact and religious fact were one and the same. It was reasonable to have faith because faith was factual. Scientific rationality thus invaded and possessed religion, and the resulting outlook responded to the rationalistic Enlightenment by itself becoming a perfect expression of it.

While religion was rearranging itself so as to appear as factual and as rational as science, a new force appeared which far from denying the identification of religion with fantasy, took it even more literally. This produced a similar rejection of fantasy on the part of religious people. This new force was psychoanalysis. In a series of brilliant studies, the first of which appeared before the First World War and the last just before the outbreak of the Second World War, Sigmund Freud showed that religious belief seemed to have all the characteristics of fantasy, and that historical and social expressions of corporate religion could best be understood as a massive extension of the same process of fantasy which was operating in the individual neurotic. Religion was thus the illusion of a sick and immature society. Freud interpreted himself as the new Moses who would lead humanity out of its primitive fears into a new reality, a liberation which would result from a more truthful view of life.

Fantasy and certitude

Using science and psychoanalysis as examples, it has been shown that religious faith in modern times has been led to overestimate its own 'facticity', and to distinguish itself too sharply from fantasy. This was, no doubt, an understandable reaction on the part of a religious tradition which was feeling deeply misunderstood by an increasingly confident and progressively enlightened scientific culture. Today, however, we are in a position to recognize this reaction as being no more than defensive. It has led to a kind of religious self-understanding which is as impoverished as the interpretations of religion offered by the burgeoning social services themselves. If history, science and psychoanalysis reduced religion to old wives' and husbands' tales, and sick imaginations, a defensively reacting religion awoke to find itself trapped in a one-dimensional world where all that could be heard were the claims and counter-claims about evidence.

Both science and religion are coming to understand themselves and each other better. The belief that science makes progress as more and more facts are accumulated has been discredited. Philosophers of science no longer believe that newly discovered facts can be used in some straightforward way to overthrow scientific theories. Facts are already theory-laden. Fact and interpretation are indissolubly linked. We now see that theory struggles against theory, and interpretation against interpretation. Scientists who continue to believe in the theoretical significance of what was once called 'fact' are becoming few indeed.

The same thing has been happening within religion. Just as theology is not usually regarded today as being a series of deductions made from revealed principles, so religious faith is less and less to be thought of as based upon conclusions drawn from facts. Revelation takes many forms and there are many kinds of facts. There are many kinds of coherence and many kinds of evidence. In both science and religion, truthfulness is now not to be reduced to a straightforward matter of verification through appeals to experience via the senses.

New movements in theology

Many of the new theological movements of our century can be understood as attempts to overthrow the old one-dimensional understanding of religious fact, and so to reintegrate the heart and body of religion around a restored and healed mind. Such tendencies can certainly be seen in the personalism of Martin Buber in the 1920s, the existentialism of Rudolf Bultmann in the 1940s and 50s, the depth theologies of Paul Tillich and Abraham Joshua Heschel in the 1950s and 60s, and the concrete, political theologies which we find in many continents today. In the 1960s and 70s narrative theology emerged as a genre of theology especially interested in using the categories of story to reinterpret religious faith. Process thought has also been very influential in both scientific and religious thinking in promoting a view of human life in a socialized nature in ways more dynamic and more relational than the older more static worlds of Newtonian physics and Victorian biblicism.

Religious education and fantasy

We can see the results of this change of air in religious education. A religious education more open towards dreams and visions will speak more vividly to children of a religious experience which comes out of the future of humanity as well as the past. What matters in religious education is not only where and how religions have come down to us, but where religions are offering to take us. When addressing suffering humanity, what religions offer are utopias not panaceas. These utopias take many forms, whether of heaven or of paradise, of nirvana or of the Kingdom of God. In every case, such visions of endless futures can best be explored through poetic images of human hope. What a frame does for the picture, the fantastic does for religious ethics. It provides a context, a horizon, a changing border beyond which everything is different, within which the demands of duty are transformed. Fantasy challenges reality in the name of hope.

The implications of this can be seen particularly when teaching the holy scriptures. The Bible, for example, has its principal educational significance not as a record of the past but as a gift to the imagination of the child. Imagination is activated in play, and teachers of young children are becoming more interested in the connections between religion and play. It is precisely in lifting from teachers the burden of a supposed orthodoxy, in freeing them from the need always to know the truth, and in encouraging a more tentative, exploratory and playful use of images that fantasy has much to offer. Instead of being too preoccupied with whether the young child can understand the religious concept, we should concentrate more on proliferating the images which the child associates with religion. The importance of laughter in the religious education of young children deserves more recognition.

The secondary pupil and social fantasy

Many critics of Western culture have pointed out that the creation of fantasy is a prominent feature of the entertainment industries. The early years of Hollywood are now the classical period in the rise of the profitable creation of fantasy. In contemporary culture, this power has now widened to include the profitable creation of entire cultures of fantasy. 'Masters of the Universe' appears not only on television, but in the sticker books, the T-shirts and even the ice-cream cones. People are lured into entire worlds, which could be dismissed as mere fad and fashion if the impact upon the imagination was not so dramatic and far-reaching. There must be many a child in Britain today whose first real experience of transcendent power has come through He-man.

In the experience of the adolescent and the adult, the border lines between the world of contrived fantasy and the actual social reality become indistinct. Instead of fantasy enclosing ethics, as we find in the religions, we have fantasy masquerading as social values. The images of men and women in public life built up by the media today are as fantastic as He-man, but less obviously so, and therefore more dangerous. The provocation of fantasy in advertising and in the stimulation of consumer desires is extremely important, and depends for its effectiveness upon remaining largely invisible. The most dangerous and pervasive fantasies are those which are so taken for granted that they appear to us to be reality itself.

Religion and the breaking of illusion

Faith development could be described as a process of continually breaking infantile illusions. This view would be the opposite to that held by Sigmund Freud. The truth probably includes both points of view: infantile religion is the religion of projected fantasies, but mature religion breaks those fantasies and brings the believer into a larger wholeness. Religious education teachers who want to take fantasy seriously should oscillate between taking fantasy very seriously and making fun of fantasy. Children and young people, as they grow in understanding of religion, will pass through periods of enclosure within fantasy followed by periods of escape from fantasy, making fun of fantasy and refantasizing their own world of meaning. The figure of Siva sums this up, for Siva is both the creator and the destroyer of fantasy.

Religious Education and Assessment

September 1972

*F*ollowing the example of the core and foundation subjects of the National Curriculum, Religious Education since the 1988 Education Reform Act has become much more sophisticated in its forms of assessment. However, this early article, inspired by the new developments in the then Certificate of Secondary Education, may still have something to offer.

Unless they assess the extent to which their pupils have learnt, teachers have no reliable way of knowing how effective their teaching has been. They do not know if they need to change their methods or to adapt the content of their lessons. Assessment of the pupil is essentially assessment of the process of education. But if the teaching and learning of religion cannot be assessed, any attempt to improve its quality can be nothing but guesswork.

Assessment and aims

It would be rather silly to try to assess the achieving of what has not even been attempted. Assessment is thus related to the aims of teaching. It is at this point that the assessment of religious education presents particular problems. If the aim is to impart knowledge of facts, whether of the Bible or of religious activities today, tests of these can easily be prepared. But if the aims include the acquisition by the pupil of insight into religion and of attitudes of tolerance and sympathy towards it, or if the development of moral qualities in the pupil is part of the aim of teaching religion, then assessment bristles with difficulties. It may be that only the trivial aspects of religious education can be assessed easily and reliably and if this is the case emphasis on assessment may encourage a teacher to concentrate upon the superficial.

Types of assessment

These problems extend beyond such things as end-of-term tests to cover a whole range of school activities. The writing of reports and references, the placing of pupils in streams and sets, and the conduct of public examinations are all part of assessment, but these various activities serve purposes wider and more complex than assessment alone. School reports are part of the image of the school which is projected towards the parents. Public examinations are a preparation for a pupil's career. It is not surprising that even within one school a teacher who thinks in pastoral terms will adopt different forms of assessment from the colleague who thinks of religious education in more subject-centred ways. Three things, however, stand out clearly in the discussion about this problem. Attempts to assess religious learning must go beyond the assessment of factual knowledge. In public examinations the assessment of religious learning must be more sharply distinguished from attempts to assess the personal faith or orthodoxy or morality of candidates. Finally, participation in the conduct of the examinations is producing a high level of sophisticated reflection on the part of the teachers concerned. This pool of teacher experience and expertise may be the most important legacy which present problems of assessment may bequeath to the future of the subject.

Chapter 3

Religious Education and Collective Worship in Policy and Practice

Religious Education in the 1988 Education Reform Act (I)

Summer 1988

I n July of 1987 the government issued a consultation document announcing its proposals to introduce a National Curriculum as the central feature of the Education Reform Bill which was to be published in November. There was alarm amongst religious educators when it was discovered that religious education was not to be included in the new compulsory curriculum, and it was generally agreed that either the subject should be included or that steps should be taken to ensure that the place of religious education would not be weakened. The following editorial, written late in 1987 and published in April the next year as the Summer issue of the journal sets out the arguments typically used at that stage of the discussion.

It seemed so simple. There was already a legal framework for the teaching of religion in school and it was working well. This framework required that religion should be taught in every county, aided and voluntary school in England and Wales, so there was no reason to add it to the list of subjects in the proposed National Curriculum. Indeed, it was not easy to see how the provision of the 1944 Act could be adapted without controversy and difficulty for the needs of the National Curriculum proposals.

This was how Kenneth Baker's policy on religious education in modern Britain took shape. All that was necessary was to remind people of the 1944 legislation. This delicate issue could then be left safely on one side.

Everybody who knew anything about religious education as it is actually practised in our schools saw things differently. The religious communities, the university departments of theology, religious studies and education, and the professional bodies concerned with religious education agreed that the effect of the proposals would be to make a neglected and marginalized subject even more severely marginalized and neglected.

Why religious education will suffer

The Department of Education and Science *Statistical Bulletin* for October 1987, 'The 1984 secondary school staffing survey; data on the curriculum in maintained secondary schools in England', reveals that in the secondary schools sampled 38 per cent of fourth-year pupils are not receiving religious education. In the fifth year this rises to 42 per cent. By way of contrast, only 5 per cent of third-year pupils are not receiving religious education. This provides dramatic confirmation of what has been known in religious education for several years. Religious education in the secondary school is increasingly concentrated into the first three years, but is rapidly disappearing in the fourth and fifth years.

It is easy to see what will happen when the attention of headteachers, governing bodies and LEAs is concentrated upon achieving success in the subjects of the National Core and Foundation Curriculum. The results of the examinations in these subjects will be made public and will determine the standing of each school. In-service priorities will be given to those subjects, additional staff will be appointed to teach them, finance will be made available for their improvement where necessary. Religious education will simply not count. Will schools encourage pupils in the third year to opt for a subject which is not going to count in the school's public image, a subject which will not contribute to the school's effectiveness in teaching the National Curriculum? Will schools make it possible for pupils in the fourth and fifth years to achieve the background of knowledge and interest in religious studies which will lead to the subject being taken at GCSE and 'A' levels? There can be no reasonable doubt about the answers to these questions and information and anecdote are flowing freely about the impact which the proposals are already having.

But, the government replies, this cannot be. Religion is a required subject under the 1944 Act. The government does not seem to realize that the 1944 Act is being more honoured in the breach than in the observance. For years those responsible for religious education have been calling for positive steps to reverse this situation of decline and indifference but the response of the government has been patchy. At the present time certain reassurances are offered. What are they?

What the government now promises

In Chapter 1, section 6(c) of the Education Bill we read the following: 'in relation to any maintained school and any school year, it shall be the duty of the local education authority and the governing body to exercise their functions with a view to securing, and the duty of the headteacher to secure ... that Section 25 (2) of the 1944 Act (compulsory religious instruction) is complied with'. It is all very well to pass laws requiring people to keep earlier laws, but if the earlier laws are already being largely disregarded what confidence can we have that this requirement will have any better result? Laws are not passed as expressions of hope but in order to bring about results. What result will this form of words have?

Again the Government has an answer: the complaints procedure is to be strengthened. It is difficult for us to interpret this. In Chapter 1 of the Bill, section 15 says that 'every local education authority shall, with the approval of the Secretary of State and after consultation with governing bodies of aided schools ... make arrangements for the consideration and disposal of any complaint....' It seems to be the intention that local committees or courts to hear complaints are to be created. The wording of the new Bill goes on to declare that unless a complaint has been through this local machinery the Secretary of State cannot deal with it.

It is this local hearing which the government regards as a strengthening of the complaints procedure. Whether this will actually be the case remains to be seen, since a great deal will depend upon how the local committee is to be created and who is to be represented upon it. There is however a more general problem created by dependence upon a complaints mechanism of whatever kind. It means that parents, teachers and others interested in religious education will have to take public and possibly embarrassing action against local friends and colleagues. This places religious education in an invidious position. While other subjects flourish naturally in the flowing river of resources and concern, religious education must moan from the parched deserts. Religious education is thrown into a negative role. In any case, it is by no means clear what kind of complaint could be legitimate. Is it a matter of complaint if there is no specialist teacher of religious education on the staff of a secondary school? Can we complain if student teachers preparing for primary schools receive no training in religious education, if an agreed syllabus has not been revised for thirty years, or if pupils receive only one period of religious education a week? The 1944 Act, it must be remembered, merely says that religious education 'shall be given'. What counts as fulfilling this has never been made clear in law. It is also likely that any changes undertaken in a school or by an LEA in response to a successful complaint will be undertaken with grudging reluctance, and will lead to a removal of resources from another area, one which is thought to have greater significance in the life of the school or the area than religious education. In other words, religious education will be placed in a double bind, because too many successful complaints will inevitably lead to a demand that section 25 (2) of the 1944 Act should be repealed.

Religious education is, indeed, faced with an ironic paradox. For many years the subject has been a little uncomfortable in its isolation as the only required subject not really required.

Will the Government *act*? Perhaps it is not too late to hope that religious education will be included in the subjects of the National Curriculum. It would be perfectly possible to do this in a way quite compatible with the existing legislation, and the various questions such as the status of the agreed syllabuses, the withdrawal clauses and denominational instruction in church-related schools can be solved. If this does not take place, the next question will be whether the government will make good its assurances, that religious education shall not suffer under the new arrangements. In this respect, various suggestions have been made. It has been said that religious education might be inspected in exactly the same way as the subjects of the National Curriculum, that the Standing Advisory Council for Religious Education, which at present any LEA may create, will become mandatory, and that a national enquiry into the present situation of religious education may be held. But will LEAs be directed to place a high priority on the secondment of teachers to religious education in-service training courses? Will resources be made available to permit curriculum development of the subject both at national and local levels? Will the government direct that every student teacher in primary school training receive adequate preparation for teaching religion?

The spirituality of education

In the new Education Bill, the spirituality of education is a major emphasis. The second paragraph of the Bill declares that the curriculum shall be satisfactory if it 'promotes the spiritual, moral, cultural, mental and physical development of pupils'. This could be a helpful emphasis, but it all depends upon the interpretation and the results. On the one hand, the emphasis upon the spiritual could mean little more than a further intrusion into education of the government's concerns for the creation of a culture appropriate to the needs of late-industrial society. In that case, spirituality will simply mean that pupils will be encouraged to become more competitive, self-assured and independent in outlook. On the other hand, it is possible that the great spiritual traditions have a part to play in the achievement of a curriculum which promotes the spiritual development of pupils. It is difficult to see how any convincing curriculum for spiritual development could be presented effectively without taking very seriously the contribution of religion. In that case, religious education must occupy a prominent position in any attempt to assess the adequacy of any school curriculum. Will the government, however, give the clause this interpretation? Will the government, having recognized the intimate connection between spiritual development and the study of religion, do something to ensure that the study of religion is actually delivered to every pupil?

It all seems so simple, and the intentions of the government are no doubt perfectly honourable. To be honourable but unrealistic is a bad combination in political life. Realism demands that positive and practical steps be taken to ensure that the government's good intentions are translated into something which will make a definite impact upon the education offered in every school. If, however, the assurances remain nothing more than that, then the result of the great Education Reform Bill is likely to be seen by later historians of education as constituting the most serious attack upon spiritual, moral and religious values in school life offered by any government this century.

Religious Education in the 1988 Education Reform Act (II)

Autumn 1988

The position of religious education and collective worship in the final form of the Education Reform Act turned out to be rather ambiguous. On the one hand, it was certainly more prominent. On the other hand, it was not clear that the prominence was altogether desirable. This extract, written early in August 1988 and published in September, was a first attempt at appraising the significance of these proposals for religious education.

In early July of 1988, the full implications of the Education Reform Bill for religious education were still unclear. The situation had been changing month by month as new amendments came before Parliament. However, when the Bill was published on 29th July, the text was available although its significance was still not clear.

The limited success of the campaign

When the Bill was first published in November of 1987 it contained only two lines dealing with religious education. If the references to religious education in the various parts of the Bill in its final stage are collated, they come to about fifteen pages. This was a striking result, and indicates the enormous interest and support which religious education commanded not only from churches and other religious groups, but from parents and teachers. What had been sought for religious education was an unambiguous place within the subjects of the National Curriculum, either as a core or as a foundation subject. What came instead was a new entity called the 'basic curriculum', consisting of religious education together with the core and foundation subjects of the National Curriculum. It was not clear how the government would interpret the basic curriculum and to what extent religious education would benefit from inclusion in it, or whether it would only suffer from exclusion from the National Curriculum. The fact that religious education was not to be within the National Curriculum on the same basis as subjects such as English, history, geography and mathematics, was a disappointment to many. The difficulties which the government saw in such an inclusion were entirely of its own making. What the Bill offered by way of a strengthening of the subject may be more than counter-balanced by the volume of resources and commitment which necessarily flow into the core and foundation subjects.

The local arrangements

While the core and foundation subjects of the National Curriculum have been strengthened at the national level, religious education will be strengthened at the local level. This will be done through the Standing Advisory Council for Religious Education (SACRE). Previously every Local Education Authority could choose whether to create such a council or not. Under the new Bill, they have to. Moreover, the SACREs are modelled upon the Conferences which produce the agreed syllabuses, comprising the four committees representing the LEA itself, the teachers and the interested religious parties. The SACRE is to be the reference point for the local complaints procedure, and has a number of other responsibilities including the interpretation of certain national requirements in the light of the local situation. It is clear that there will be some central government funding for the subjects of the National Curriculum, but that the SACREs might be dependent upon local government finance. More important still, perhaps, is the question of the preparation and training of the people who will comprise the new SACREs. The central problem is whether the people who represent the religious denominations and will control two of the four committees will look upon their task as being primarily an education one, or will think of themselves as being mainly the representatives and custodians of the religious denominations. Indeed the question of the educational responsibility of the religions has emerged as one of the most important factors in the whole situation.

The value of a minimum definition

Religious education in England and Wales owes a great deal of its achievement to the fact that there has been a minimum definition of the subject, both in its classroom work and in its place in the school assembly. The subject was known simply as Religious Instruction or (in the case of the nineteenth-century assembly) Religious Observances. Legislators in 1870 and again in 1944 showed courage in resisting the demands of partisan interests that a more specific definition should be adopted. It was this low profile of definition which enabled the subject to adapt to changing theological and social emphasis, avoided unpleasant political and legal wrangles over theology, put the responsibility clearly in the hands of those closest to the classroom, and enabled religious education to perform valuable bridge-building functions.

This had come to fruition in the last twenty or twenty-five years, in that religious education was able to win the confidence of a wide spectrum of opinion and so to launch the unique British experience of multi-faith dialogue in the classroom. The educational and social consequences of this enlightened policy had won worldwide interest and admiration. It seemed to be attracting increasing support as the most responsible policy available to those churches with a commitment to education in the county schools.

This was overthrown in 1988 by a combination of forces, the exact nature of which requires careful analysis. It is too early to assess the exact implications which the Christianizing amendments will have for the agreed syllabuses and for school assembly. It is clear, however, that these amendments, which thrust Christianity into a position of embarrassing prominence, are contrary to the British tradition, are not easily compatible with educational principles, are difficult to defend theologically, and seem unlikely to promote a society in which sympathetic acceptance and mutual understanding mark the relations between different religions and communities.

All this is done in the name of Christianity. There are Christians who seem to think that social and educational policies can be made more Christian simply by including the word. Although the early Christians complained that they were persecuted merely for the name 'Christian', there seem to be some contemporary Christians for whom the name is the all-important thing. There will, however, continue to be Christians no less committed and no less informed about their faith who will be unhappy about the imposition of Christian supremacy through legislation.

The fact that in the third reading of the Bill in the House of Lords an amendment was passed enabling pupils belonging to religions other than Christianity to hold their own separate acts of collective worship is no comfort. It is, of course, necessary to make some provision in order to avoid the situation where large groups of pupils would be withdrawn from the 'Christian' main assembly, but such a withdrawal would not be necessary had the schools been permitted to continue with the minimal definition of worship, as before. To advance the claims of one religion implies the granting of rights to the others, but providing for separate communities is no substitute for the creation of a corporate life of mutual understanding. It is not enough to respect each other's points of view; we must learn to share each other's lives and to participate in each other's hopes.

The Content of Religious Education as Required by Law

Spring 1989

The wording of section 8(3) of the 1988 Education Reform Act is certainly more ambiguous than was at first realized. As time has passed, the pluralistic interpretation, which saw section 8(3) as supporting the world religions syllabuses of former years has gathered strength and is now generally recognized. Professor Robert Jackson, for example, in his 1997 book Religious Education; an interpretative approach *(London, Hodder & Stoughton) says that 'many religious educators internationally look with particular interest at England and Wales, since the 1988 Education Reform Act, for the first time in law, stated that religious education had to give attention to the Religious Plurality of the nation'. The following article was one of the earliest to point out the plural implications for the new agreed syllabuses.*

One of the most significant features of the new Education Act is that religious instruction has been abolished. In section 1(1) ('The Curriculum') we are told that the authorities responsible for the schools shall 'exercise their functions (including in particular the functions conferred on them by this chapter with respect to religious education, religious worship and the National Curriculum)'.

This is the first time in law that religion taught in the classrooms in England and Wales has been called 'religious education'. The expression used in Acts of Parliament from 1870 to 1944 was 'religious instruction'. The expression 'religious education' has been increasing in popularity steadily during the previous fifty or sixty years. It was widely felt that the word 'instruction' suggested something too narrow, too authoritarian, and too suggestive of the transmission of a set body of knowledge or doctrine. Well before 1944 many religious educators were calling for the word 'instruction' to be abandoned. Dr Basil Yeaxlee, in his 1931 series of lectures to teachers *The Approach to Religious Education*, had already described the continued use of the expression 'religious instruction' as an example of bureaucratic rigidity, and as completely failing to express the 'enquiring and life-enriching' process which the teaching of religion in schools demanded. In trying to get away from the rigidity of an imposed instruction, many agreed syllabuses were already describing themselves as being educational. The famous Yorkshire West Riding Syllabus of 1966 used the title *Suggestions for Religious Education*. It was something of a shock when the 1975 Birmingham Agreed Syllabus reverted to the use of the legal expression 'religious instruction' but this was because of the lively discussion about the interpretation of the 1944 Act which was going on at that time.

The change, therefore, from instruction to education in the new Act is long overdue and comes as no surprise. It is, nevertheless, of some significance.

Instruction is a content-centred process, which consists of the transmission of knowledge from the teacher to the pupil. Education is a person-centred process which aims at human development.

Balanced and broadly based

The move from instruction to education is consistent with the description of the nature of the school curriculum which follows in section 1(2). 'The curriculum for a maintained school satisfies the requirements of this section if it is a balanced and broadly based curriculum.' Religious education, in fulfilment of this ideal, is itself to be balanced and broadly based. It was the humanists who introduced the word 'balanced' into discussions about religious education in the middle and late 1970s, and it is good to see this emphasis coming now officially into the religious education curriculum. The word 'balanced' suggests that there is more than one aspect, more than one kind of material, several emphases and perspectives. This is consistent with the expression 'broadly-based'.

The purpose of this balanced and broadly-based curriculum is to promote 'the spiritual, moral, cultural, mental and physical development of pupils and of society'. It is important to notice that the development of society is a goal of the curriculum. The spiritual and cultural development of society at large is to be promoted by means of a balanced and broadly based curriculum.

Here we have a starting point from which the religious provisions of the 1988 Education Act are to be interpreted. Religious education is to be more educational and less instructional. It is to be broad and balanced, not narrow and authoritarian. It is to be developmental, taking spiritual and cultural factors into account.

Continuity rather than change

Many people have emphasized the changes which the Act requires, but it would be easy to exaggerate these. Most educational legislation gives legal sanction and official support for what schools have long been doing. This was the case in 1944. Agreed syllabuses, for example, were not created by the 1944 Act. They had been in great popularity during the 1920s and 1930s and the Act merely ratified and clarified their use, making mandatory what previously had been done for purely professional reasons.

The 1988 Act is no exception. There are certainly changes and some of them are important, but the major emphasis is upon continuity. This is apparent in section 8 where the special provisions for religious education are set out. The first thing that is said about religious education here was that it should be 'of the kind required by such of the provisions of sections 26 to 28 of the 1944 Act ... as apply in the case of that school'. This means that religious education shall be given to all pupils in attendance at the school, and shall be given in accordance with an Agreed Syllabus. The 1944 Act did not say that only pupils under the school leaving age should receive religious education; the law applied to pupils in *schools* not to pupils of a certain age. The new Act makes it perfectly clear that this was indeed the intention, and it is now clear that pupils in sixth forms of schools must all receive religious education as part of their basic curriculum.

The agreed syllabuses

It is because of this insistence that the religious education required by the 1988 Baker Act should be like that required by the 1944 Butler Act that the emphasis has been placed upon agreed syllabuses. Religious education is basic but it is not national. The agreed syllabuses which have been such a successful feature of religious education are here re-emphasized. Although the agreed syllabuses are local – and this is one of the reasons why religious education is not regarded as being part of the National Curriculum in a formal sense – local in administration and control does not mean local in content. The content is to be typical of Great Britain.

Here we have something completely new. In previous legislation, a low definition of religion and of religious education (instruction) was provided. In the 1988 Act more specific definition of the content of the agreed syllabuses is provided. Section 8(3) reads: 'any agreed syllabus which after this section comes into force is adopted or deemed to be adopted ... shall reflect the fact that the religious traditions in Great Britain are in the main Christian whilst taking account of the teaching and practices of the other principal religions represented in Great Britain.'

It is important to realize that this requirement will apply only to new agreed syllabuses. If an LEA does not adopt a new syllabus, the impact of the new Education Act upon the content of religious education will be precisely nil. There has been much misunderstanding of this point. The new Act does not require any direct change in the content of religious education at all. This is a result of the decision to work through the vehicle of the agreed syllabus conference at the local level.

In the case of new agreed syllabuses, however, there is a clear description of the required content. The description is balanced, as section 1 already indicated, in that the requirement falls into two halves, the first dealing with Christianity and the second dealing with the other principal religious traditions. A balanced religious education curriculum must thus be a multi-faith curriculum. There is absolutely no suggestion here that religious education should be 'Christian-based', 'Christian-centred' or should offer an undue emphasis upon Christianity. The first half of the requirement is introduced by the expression 'shall reflect the fact that' and the second half is introduced with the words 'whilst taking account of'. These expressions seem to indicate a balanced approach.

We thus see that no syllabus based upon Christianity alone can, any longer, be a legal syllabus. Many of the older agreed syllabuses, compiled during the 1940s and 1950s but still in force, do concentrate almost entirely upon Christianity, and it is this group of syllabuses which will be in most need of revision. We may say that the requirement of the new Act breaks the assumed Christian monopoly (never required by law) which was the practice of most of the old agreed syllabuses.

Moreover, religious education is not to be taught from the point of view of biblical origins, as was so often the case thirty years ago, but from the point of view of the living religious traditions of the present time. This represents a considerable acknowledgment of the work done in the last twenty years in turning the interest of religious education upon contemporary religion as a living reality.

In the wording of this section, Christianity is regarded as one of a class. The class is 'the religious traditions in Great Britain' and of these Christianity is regarded as the principal group. The plurality of Christianity is acknowledged, since the wording does not speak of the Christian religious tradition but of the religious traditions which are Christian. It is thus clear that the old-fashioned practice of presenting Christianity as a unified entity must disappear. Full weight must be given to the range and variety of Christian religious traditions.

In the case of the other principal religious traditions in Great Britain, the new syllabuses must take account of both their teaching and their practices. We see thus that the doctrine (i.e. the teaching) of several religions becomes an integral part of religious education. Once again, the Act is supporting what has become the practice in the agreed syllabuses of the past fifteen years or so.

The significance of this emphasis upon plurality must be emphasized. A traditional feature of many agreed syllabuses has been the local history of Christianity. It has sometimes been argued that in counties where Christianity is virtually the only religious tradition there was no point in including the teaching and practices of Islam and Hinduism. Such a position will no longer be valid, since the new Act requires each local agreed syllabus to take account not so much of the religious traditions present in the locality but those represented in Great Britain. On any reckoning, Judaism, Islam, Hinduism, the Sikh faith and Buddhism are major religious traditions which are represented in Great Britain. Whether or not they are religious traditions *of* Great Britain is not the point. They do not have to be. They are certainly principal religions *represented* in Great Britain and no agreed syllabus will meet the requirements of this section of the Act unless it takes into account their teaching and practices.

The truth and the rhetoric

Many people have got the impression that the new Act announces a period of Christian aggression in education. Alarm has been expressed by thoughtful Muslims, Jews and others about the effects of this upon religious harmony in this country. The fact is that the Act gives no support whatsoever to Christian supremacy in the classroom. It is true that Christianity is mentioned on the face of the Bill while the other principal religions are only mentioned as a group, but placed in the context of the educational emphasis which religious teaching is to have, this represents no more than official support for the curriculum development which has been going on in religious education in recent years. Misguided Christians who are inspired more by tribalistic enthusiasm than by a responsible Christian concern for the Kingdom of God in Britain today must be gently but persistently reminded of the actual wording of the new Act.

Conclusions

We have not here been addressing what legislation the country should have for religious education, but what it does have. This has not been a philosophical argument but a series of practical suggestions. We still take the view that religious education would be better without this high definition of content, and that in the long run Butler will prove to have been wiser than Baker in this respect. Be that as it may, the Act is now with us, and it is important to realize what it really says. It must also be added that just because the Act emphasizes continuity in the classroom teaching of religion, there is no need to suppose that it will not be followed by a new wave of curriculum development. This happened in the late 1940s and we may expect that it will again take place in the wake of this new Act. One of the greatest possibilities which the Act holds for religious education is that by focusing public and professional attention upon religious education it will highlight many areas of neglect and will lead to better provision. The syllabuses of the 1970s, even though confirmed by the wording of the new Act, are not necessarily the best available for tomorrow's children. If the Act stimulates new work in the teaching of both Christianity and other religions, it will be all to the good.

'Mish-mash': Religious Education and Pluralism

Summer 1990

The following article was later expanded into my booklet Mishmash: Religious Education in a multi-cultural Britain: a study in metaphor *(Derby, CEM, 1991). In spite of the fact that I was able to demonstrate that the expression 'mish-mash' and other similar metaphors of disgusting food mixtures used by the Christian religionists to disparage religious education spring from a desire for an élitist social and cognitive purity, use of such expressions still continues. Those who do not like to have contact with people and ideas other than their own, can hardly help reacting in this way, so strong is the disgust and apprehension which they feel at the possibility of the breaking-down of social and religious barriers. Unfortunately, the so-called model syllabuses published by the School Curriculum and Assessment Authority (SCAA) in 1994 are consistent with the idea that religions should be taught in separate compartments. At the local level, people from various communities have had the good sense to realize that they need to live together in understanding and mutual acceptance, and, therefore, nearly all the local agreed syllabuses make provision for studies of religions which cross religious frontiers.*

Towards the end of this study, I make the claim that the law does not permit children studying an agreed syllabus to be separated from one another in religious groups. This perhaps requires a further word of explanation. The law provides for an agreed syllabus of religious education which shall be taught to all the pupils in the school, subject only to the right of the parents to withdraw their children. The law does not expressly forbid the presentation of the teaching to children gathered in separate religious groups, but this would clearly be contrary to the spirit and expectation of the legislation. Religious education is to be taught in accordance with an agreed syllabus. All the major groups in the community are expected to work together in order to reach this agreement. It would be inconsistent with this practice if, having agreed together, a religious group then broke away and insisted that their children should receive the agreed syllabus education separately from the other children. Moreover, the fact that the law prevents denominational instruction in favour of a more general religious education also suggests that children are to receive a common education. What purpose could there be in a separate religious education, other than to present children with the distinctive teachings of that religion? It is clear then that the very conception of the agreed syllabuses is inconsistent with the idea of separate syllabuses for each religious group (the religions would then not have reached an agreement about a syllabus) or with the teaching of this agreed syllabus to pupils divided along religious grounds.

If we read the reports of the 1988 Parliamentary debates on religious education, one word stands out as summarizing that feature which was perceived as being most in need of reform: mish-mash. But what is mish-mash? It would not be correct to say that it refers simply to the fact that religious education deals with a number of religions. The protest is not directed against the teaching of world religions as such.

Summing up the debates in the House of Lords on 27th July 1988, one of the members said that what had happened had been 'an inter-faith effort to secure the individuality and respect of all religions'. Again and again it is emphasized that other religions apart from Christianity are significant, must be respected and taught in school. 'In our country there are situations in which it is right to acknowledge that there are those of other faiths and to ensure that proper instruction is given to them' (Col. 718, 21st June).

It is a fundamental principle 'that all religious education, Christian or otherwise, should promote respect, tolerance and understanding for those who adhere to other faiths' (Col. 659, 21st June). It would not be fair to the quality of these debates to say that they display prejudice towards religions other than Christianity or a disregard for the rights of non-Christian children. The participants in the debate made frequent references to views of the leaders of the non-Christian religions and always spoke of them with consideration. Mish-mash does not imply that religious education should consist of nothing but Christianity.

Mish-mash and the multi-faith approach

At an early stage in the debates we learn that there is a close connection between mish-mash and multi-faith religious education. We hear of 'subtle changes which undermine the Christian nature of worship in the form of multi-faith initiatives' (Col. 1345, 12th May). 'We do not offer to Muslims the opportunity to share in some mish-mash act of worship, all put together in some meaningless contrivance.' But what was it precisely about the multi-faith approach which earned the contemptuous description 'mish-mash'? As we have seen, it was not the mere teaching of several faiths. Multi-faith does not simply mean that religious education includes a multitude of faiths. That is not the point.

As the Bill went through its various stages, the principal debaters focused more sharply on what exactly would be necessary if mish-mash was to be avoided. On 21st June an early attempt was made to define the nature of a multi-faith agreed syllabus. 'It provides for a flexibility of emphasis in areas where the vast majority of pupils are from other faiths' (Col. 630). The idea seems to have been that an agreed syllabus would in most parts of the country be based on Christianity, but where necessary would be able to offer something else. It was because of this that the Bishop of London could say at this stage. 'I believe this package could signal the end of what has been described in this House as the 'mish-mash' approach to religious education' (Col. 640).

From this time on, the attempt to clarify the nature of mish-mash concentrated on the expression 'in the main, Christian'. What was meant by 'mainly'? The hope is expressed that 'this is not intended to be an endorsement of the multi-faith approach' (Col. 642). These words might be the mandate 'for some confusing multi-faith assembly'. We soon learn that one of the central characteristics of the multi-faith approach is not only to do with the nature of the content of religious education, but has to do with purifying the composition of the classes. The central concern is 'that Christian children should be taught the Christian faith and should have their own Christian collective act of worship. The second principle is that children who adhere to other faiths ... should be taught other faiths and have respectively their own collective acts of worship' (Col. 653, 21st June). In accordance with this principle of separate religious groups, 'there should be no multi-faith collective act of worship for all children irrespective of the faith to which they adhere' (Col. 659).

Later in the same debate the Bishop of London offered a further clarification of the concept of 'in the main'. He distinguished between the descriptive use of the expression in describing the agreed syllabus provisions, and the prescriptive use of the expression in requiring a certain kind of collective worship. Descriptively, the religious traditions of Great Britain are, indeed, in the main Christian. But worship should spring out of belief. It is convictual or confessional in a way that does not apply to the descriptions of the religious studies approach, and the belief out of which school worship springs will be, in the main, Christian. 'The phrase "in the main" means that account can be taken of the needs in particular localities. However, the overall requirement is necessary' (Col. 666). So we see that in other places, other schools perhaps or in other acts of collective worship, the worship may spring from some belief other than Christianity.

But what was the implication of these exceptional areas? Members of the House wanted further clarification. If that is all there is to it, some noble Lords insisted, 'it inevitably means "mish-mash" ' (Col. 713). For example, if there were areas where there were rather a lot of Jews then apparently we would still have *mainly* a Christian education 'but tuned over a little to the Jewish side'. That will not do, for 'if there is a large Jewish population they would much prefer those pupils to have a Jewish education' (Col. 713).

The approach outlined so far by the Bishop of London would surely mean that where there was a mixed population then you must have 'a degraded educational approach' (Col. 713). The Bishop replied that 'in the main' does not mean 'mainly' (Col. 717). 'It does not mean that there will be a percentage of Christian teaching spread throughout the country with a proportion of other faiths. It means what it says, which means that in the main, looking at the country as a whole, with its present multi-cultural composition, the bulk of it will be Christian. The norm will be Christian ... but there will be exceptions because of local areas, and what is proper to them in the educational setting. That is what we mean by "mainly" not mainly in the sense of two-thirds rice and one-third tapioca or something like that. This provision is not in this sense a mish-mash at all. It is a matter of applying it directly to the situation in the country' (Col. 717).

The argument here is hard to follow, as the ensuing debate soon revealed. The idea seems not to be that there will be not an invariable ratio of fixed proportions throughout the country. There will be no national mish-mash, but account will be taken of local needs. But would not the syllabuses in these local areas, if we think of the Jewish example cited, be examples of mish-mash?

Soon the solution appears. The agreed syllabus is to be produced in association with the local Standing Advisory Council on Religious Education (SACRE). One of the four representative groups of the SACRE is to be a multi-faith group. 'They are in a position to produce within the syllabus that part of it which will be applied for those children ... So if there was a majority of Christian children, there would be a Christian syllabus and a Christian form of worship which is not "in the main" Christian but Christian. That is what happens *in the main*' (Cols. 719/720). 'The multi-faith representatives on SACRE will be able to provide a balanced syllabus for children who were not Christians. This is not a mish-mash. It is exactly the reverse' (Col. 721). As for the minority who will always remain in most classrooms, whatever the syllabus, the answer is simple. They will be withdrawn.

Now at last the situation becomes clearer. One speaker remarks that he had been worried, '... because my impression was that one hundred per cent of any one religion would not be taught to children of that religion but that all children would, in the main, be taught Christianity and *also* be taught other religions' (Col. 720). The same situation applies to the acts of collective worship. The words 'in the main' apply to 'what is normal' (Col. 856). 'It does not mean that a service, or a course of instruction, is partly Christian and partly something else. It means that it is usually Christian but sometimes something else' (Col. 856, 22nd June).

How to avoid a mish-mash

It is now clear what we have to do in order to avoid a mish-mash. Both content and pupils must be strictly separated along religious lines. There must be no mixture either of persons or of teaching. The lines between one faith and another must be sharply drawn in human relations, learning situations and lesson content.

If we ask how, in such a situation, can pupils be helped to acquire tolerance and understanding of other people's faiths, the answer seems to be that the innate demand of each great world faith for love and respect for the neighbour will suffice. What is required is a situation of parallel instruction, in which each group is aligned vertically, beneath the teachings of its own religion. There must be no horizontal links. There must be no mutuality, no sharing of the ideals and hopes of the other, no dialogue. In most parts of the country, agreed syllabuses will be totally Christian. Small minorities of inappropriate children can be withdrawn. Where the numbers of such inappropriate children are too great for withdrawal, a syllabus must be provided which will have separate sections appropriate for each of these religious groups. The Hindus will study the Hindu section, the Muslims the Muslim section and so on. Alternatively, the idea might be that in a mixed local area several syllabuses might be produced, each one dealing separately and distinctly with the children from one particular religious tradition.

The horror of mixing

It is remarkable how strongly some of the noble Lords felt about this matter. It emerges as their principal concern. The results of mixing are described in quite powerful terms, often using metaphors taken from food and drink or from purity taboos. One is reminded quite strongly of the writings of the anthropologist Mary Douglas in, for example, *Natural Symbols,* where the relationships between ritual purity and the symbolism of the orifices of the body are brilliantly described.

In syllabuses which draw upon several religions, 'all faiths are trivialised, and faith itself may be destroyed'. There will then be a need 'to protect the integrity of Christianity and of other world religions' (Col. 641, 21st June). Multi-faith approaches are 'confusing' (Col. 642) and lead to 'the destruction of the purity of worship'. 'The Christian faith should be taught undiluted ... it should not be muddled by trying to teach it with overtones of something else infiltrated into it' (Col. 659). Mixing will lead to 'a degraded educational approach' (21st June).

The danger of contagion

According to this approach, it is in the best interests of all religions that they should not have contact with each other. Development must be equal but separate. Religious education, in this view, would create a sort of spiritual apartheid, and would be organized like a series of isolation wards, with carefully constructed barriers to prevent cross-infection or (even worse) cross-fertilization.

There is something deeply Protestant about this view of the relations between religions. Johann Baptist Metz has discussed this in his book *The Emergent Church, the future of Christianity in a postbourgeois world* (London, SCM Press, 1981). 'The Reformation's fear of sin, became, by gradual degrees, another kind of fear. I call this "fear of contact", fear of contacting what is of the earth, of the senses, of that bodily, social life within which grace wishes to bestow itself upon us....' Metz traces this fear of contagion back to what he calls 'the pathos of pure doctrine', in which the Church sought for 'pure doctrine' against the contaminated, worldly and depraved religious life of late-medieval society. The world came to be seen as infected with evil compromises. Now, the idea of the 'pure' has become bound up with the inward, the spiritual, the non-sensual. It is a kind of Christianity which tries to convince us that grace is mediated through faith only, through the pure teaching. There is nothing to be touched or handled, and there is a constant threat that close contact will adulterate the integrity of the faith. This in turn bred a fear of becoming enmeshed in 'impure, contradictory social conflicts' (pp. 51f.).

Whenever we are contemplating a change in religious education we need to ask whether it takes us nearer to the separated communities of Belfast and Beirut or nearer to the life of love. There is no doubt that the social expression of the view of the syllabus which we have been discussing is the ghetto.

From the educational point of view, the recommended policy would also be unacceptable. This model of parallel, uncritical instruction must be clearly distinguished from models of dialogical education. One of the major features of the educational experience, the enlarging of cognitive perspective, would be lost if we were to adopt the separatist approach.

Moreover, this approach is profoundly unscientific, since it denies the common realities of religion. All the major world faiths present features which are unique and features which are shared. The history of religions shows that we are not dealing with separate, static blocks of material, but with a dynamic process of mutual influencing.

From the psychological point of view, it is hard to see how intelligent and lively pupils can be boxed-up in instructional separation. There is a natural curiosity about the lives and beliefs of others, which if denied must lead to frustration and apathy. Fundamentally, the separatist approach is a kind of Sunday school system. The next step would be to have the classes instructed by priests and other representatives of the religion in question; indeed this was suggested more than once during the debates. The potential of religious education to work in flexible and integrated ways with other subject areas would be undercut.

One of the contributors to the attack upon the wider approach summed up the situation quite clearly. 'At the end of the day, it will mean subordinating much of our own culture. We shall end up not just with a mish-mash of religious education but with a mish-mash of almost everything else, including history and geography' (Col. 684, 21st June).

The outcome

A number of peers continued to express their doubts very late in the proceedings. They were convinced about the intention of the Bishop of London to avoid mish-mash, but they did not think that the form of words proposed to them would do the job. In this respect, they were correct. The requirements for the new agreed syllabuses do not state that they must reflect the fact that the principal religious traditions in Great Britain are in the main Christian and *where appropriate* take account of the teaching and practices of the other principal religions represented in Great Britain. Each and every new agreed syllabus is to do both things. In areas where there is a great majority of pupils from religions other than Christianity, the agreed syllabus must still reflect the general Christian situation throughout Great Britain, in a manner no doubt appropriate to the needs of the community, and in areas where there are few members of other faiths the syllabus must nevertheless take account of their teachings and practices. The wording not only does not require pupils and content to be separated religion by religion; it does not permit it.

As for multi-faith collective worship, a number of LEAs, including the London Boroughs of Ealing and Brent, together with Bradford and Birmingham, have now given permission to many schools to construct multi-faith collective worship. There is no other acceptable community policy.

The horror of mish-mash is the horror of a threatened identity. Religious education must play its part in widening identity from the tribe and from the nation to all that is truly human.

The Religious Education Clauses of the 1993 Education Act

Summer 1993

This article was written in March of 1993, when there was a brisk controversy regarding the religious education and reflective clauses of the 1993 Education Bill. No attempt has been made to bring this entry up to date. Its interest lies in the light it throws on the character of the discussions, and this in turn enables teachers and others to interpret the situation of religious education today. I have described the beliefs and attitudes of the Christian right wing in greater detail in my article 'A critique of Christian religionism in recent British education' *in Jeff Astley and Leslie J. Francis (eds),* Christian Theology and Religious Education: connections and contradictions *(London, SPCK, 1996, pp. 140–65).*

Throughout the autumn and spring of 1992–3 there has been a good deal of discussion about the religious education clauses of the latest Education Bill, which will be passing through the House of Lords in April and May. Discussion has focused upon the provisions made for religious education and collective worship in the 1988 Education Reform Act. The question is whether these are working or not.

The reference to Christianity

One of the striking features of the 1988 legislation was that for the first time in England and Wales the content of new agreed syllabuses was positively indicated. It is well known that in the previous Acts (for example, the 1944 Education Act) nothing had been said about the positive content of religious education other than that it was to be taught 'in accordance with an agreed syllabus'. In 1988 it was decided that new agreed syllabuses should 'reflect the fact that the principal religious traditions in Great Britain are in the main Christian whilst taking account of the teaching and practices of the other principal religions represented in Great Britain' (Section 8(3)).

Two points of view have emerged in the discussion since 1988. On one hand, there are those who maintain that the 1988 wording has created an anomaly in that one religion is referred to by name while the rest are lumped together as 'other principal religions'. It is being said that this is a licence for discrimination, has encouraged some militant Christian groups to adopt a 'Christendom' mentality, has marginalized children from Hindu, Jewish, Muslim, Sikh and other religious traditions, and has created an uneasy sense of competition between religions for space in the curriculum. It might also be said, from the strictly educational point of view, that the reference to a single religion has created the impression that religious education curricula should present religions in blocks, i.e. first one religion is taught and then the next and so on. Moreover, the wording has encouraged a revival in the instructional approach to religious education since the religious traditions have been encouraged to see themselves as the sponsors of that part of the curriculum which deals with them, one by one.

From the cluster of criticisms has emerged an interesting suggestion: the new agreed syllabuses 'should reflect the teaching and practices of the principal religions represented in Great Britain'. Just that, and no more. At a stroke this would resolve all the difficulties created by the specific reference to Christianity and would restore a position where harmonious relations between religions in an educational context could be worked out at the local level.

More Christianity?

The other point of view is that there should be yet more teaching of Christianity. It is suggested that the 1988 wording was not entirely satisfactory and has lent itself to the encouragement of a world religions approach, which (it is said) was not the intention of Parliament at the time. There are those who advocate some 'clarification' of the 1988 words, preferably in the new legislation or, failing that, through new directives to be issued by the Department for Education. This group would like new agreed syllabuses to be 'predominantly Christian' or 'mainly Christian'. They would like to secure this by the introduction of some percentage requirement, such that new agreed syllabuses would have to devote, say, 70, 80, or even 90 per cent to Christianity.

Needless to say, this point of view arouses alarm in Hindus, Jews, Muslims and others, who see it as a threat to their whole position in the educational system. It is also opposed by the religious education community which is almost unanimous on this point. Recent statements issued by the Religious Education Council of England and Wales, the Professional Council for Religious Education, the University Conference of Religious Education Lecturers and the Professional Religious Education Group have expressed concern about the educational and community relations consequences should yet more emphasis upon Christianity be required in religious education.

Who then supports the 'more Christianity' point of view? It must be said that this emphasis comes from a small and unrepresentative group of militant Christians who do not have the support of any major church group or professional association. It is noteworthy that in their various pronouncements, the names of the same three or four individuals continually recur, and although there seem to be a number of tiny organizations promulgating this point of view, the same half dozen individuals always seem to be behind them. The influence of this group is thus out of all proportion to its significance. It is unfortunate that this group tends to get rather a lot of press coverage, and it is sad that the press are attracted by the sensational and often outrageous attacks upon religious education made by the group. Governors and headteachers are getting heartily sick of reading in the press that they are flouting the law, disregarding God, Christ and the Bible and other absurd allegations, always quoting statements issued by the same three or four people.

What should be done?

On the whole, the 1988 form of words should remain for the time being. In its emphasis on the principal spiritual tradition of Britain it catches the mood of the moment, and meets a real sense of moral vacuum. The second clause requires that children should also learn from other great religions and the wording as a whole is sufficiently flexible to enable a variety of interpretations so as to meet local community needs and the needs of those schools where there is a large majority of pupils from a particular religion. It is this flexibility which is particularly valuable, and has made it possible for the schools to live with this legislation. Take away the flexibility by tighter legislation or more stringent requirements from the Department, and all kinds of controversy and opposition will certainly break out. It may be true that the emphasis on one religion is open to certain misunderstandings, but those misunderstandings have been exacerbated by the activities of the Christian extremists. Left to themselves, in the context of the local SACREs and agreed syllabus conferences, it is likely that the religious representatives and the teachers' groups will work pretty well together under the general aegis of the 1988 wording. Our message to Parliament and the DfE is clear: do nothing on this matter.

Collective worship

The same general considerations apply to section 7 of the 1988 Education Reform Act. The wording is sufficiently flexible to meet the needs of many kinds of school and, if interpreted broadly, can enable schools to hold their communities together. It is a pity that militant and unrepresentative groups of Christians have tried to use section 7 to impose on schools a tight and exclusive control. Fortunately, all these attempts have failed. On 26th February 1993, a judge of the high court dismissed a request for a judicial review of the rejection by the Secretary of State of a complaint against the Crowcroft Park Primary School in Manchester. It was thus held that the school was within the law in interpreting the 1988 Act in such a way as to include materials drawn from all the spiritual traditions represented in the community. The way seems clear for a broad and flexible interpretation of the legislation to continue.

However, the situation is fragile. The little Christian groups are now dissatisfied with the collective worship legislation of 1988 because it has failed them in their sectarian purposes. They want it to be reformed again or clarified yet more. This could be done quite easily by removing the words which offer the possibility of a broader interpretation. For example, section 7 requires worship to be 'wholly or mainly of a broadly Christian character'. If the words 'or mainly' were deleted, much of the possibility of wider interpretation would be removed. Similarly, if the clause which says that schools only have to have this kind of school worship on a majority of days of the school term were removed, there would also be a tightening up of Christian requirements. These excisions, simple though they appear to be, would have disastrous results. Schools would increasingly become places of religious rivalry and separation. Unity in the bonds of peace would be threatened.

The collective worship legislation is not the strongest part of the 1988 Act. It might be helpful in the next year or two to have a properly constituted enquiry into its working and effects. It may be that the attempt to provide a heightened theological profile for collective worship in county schools was not appropriate. In the meanwhile, the message is the same as before. On this matter, do nothing.

The Fundamental Distinction

Spring 1994

This is part of a larger study entitled 'The Fundamental Distinction: A Review of DfE Draft Circular X/94 Religious Education and Collective Worship, 11th October, 1993' which was circulated privately in November 1993. When the circular was published on 31st January 1994, the cruder expressions, which had made it vulnerable to criticism, had been mostly smoothed out, but the spirit and intention were unchanged. I accordingly modified my own discussion which was issued privately in March 1994 under the heading 'The Fundamental Distinction: A Review of DfE Circular X/94 Religious Education and Collective Worship 31st January, 1994'. At the time of writing, this circular remains in force. Part of the following editorial appeared in my article 'The Theology of the Department for Education' in Education Now Review (Vol. 47, No. 3, November 1995, pp. 243–5), (the 1993 Hockerill Lecture). The views of the government changed considerably after the General Election on 1st May 1997. However, as long as Circular 1/94 remains in force its basic pre-suppositions will continue to influence teachers.

On 11th October 1993 the DfE issued a draft of its circular X/94 *Religious Education and Collective Worship* which is expected to be made available in its final form early in 1994. It will replace Circular 3/89 in which the religious education and collective worship legislation up to that point was summarized.

As it stands at present, the new draft circular is a deeply flawed document. Its weaknesses lie in three main areas. First, it is unacceptable from the legal and administrative point of view. Secondly, as an educational document it is ill-informed and misguided. Thirdly, it rests upon a theological approach to the Christian faith which is questionable.

Legal and administrative objections

The religious education and collective worship clauses of the 1988 Education Reform Act are ambiguous. They are open to a number of interpretations. The result is that a wide variety of agreed syllabuses would be consistent with the law. The legal view seems to be that the wording is so vague that unless an agreed syllabus contains considerable detail (an aspect not specified by the law itself) it would be difficult, if not impossible, for the courts to tell whether or not a syllabus met the requirements of the law. Taking the wording of section 8(3) at face value and reading the words in their ordinary sense it would be true to say that there is not a single agreed syllabus in force today, or one published during the past twenty years, which fails to meet its requirements. The government, however, is not content with this situation.

When it became clear that diverse interpretations were possible, an attempt was made to use the 1993 Education Act to tighten up the legislation. Members of Parliament, the teachers and the faith groups were, however, not to be caught napping this time as they were in 1988. Apart from one or two slightly silly bits, the 'clarifying' amendments were all withdrawn. There was now only one hope left: to secure through departmental pressure that which had not been secured through the parliamentary process. This is why in its draft circular the DfE insists upon an interpretation of religious education and collective worship which is far more restricting than that actually permitted by the law.

It is typical of the approach of the Department that it regards most of the new agreed syllabuses prepared since 1988 as defective. There is absolutely no basis for this criticism. The now notorious review of the new agreed syllabuses carried out by the National Curriculum Council and published earlier in 1993 admits that the legislation is so vague that it is not possible to tell whether the agreed syllabuses comply with the law or not until the Department should issue fresh guidelines. In that situation, one would have expected that a reasonable Department would have issued guidelines illustrating a range of possible syllabuses, all of which would be adequate in the light of the law. Instead, they have decided to insist upon one narrow interpretation and now we are promised model agreed syllabuses in which this interpretation will be hammered home. The model syllabuses, like the draft circular, are simply techniques whereby a powerful pressure group is seeking to achieve its purposes in spite of the law.

This policy of narrow interpretation is particularly damaging in the sections of the draft circular which refer to collective worship. The older legislators had wisely refrained from theological definition, leaving it to the schools to decide what worship should be. In 1988 there was a heightened theological definition of collective worship. It was to be 'wholly or mainly of a broadly Christian character' and this in turn was to be determined by seeing whether the collective worship reflected 'the broad traditions of Christian belief'. However, the 1988 legislation (section 7) added so many ifs and buts that the end product created a somewhat convoluted and ambiguous situation.

Once again, however, instead of maximizing the freedom of interpretation which the law offers, the Department proposes a theological clarification, so to speak, which places school worship on a specific doctrinal and confessional basis which is unprecedented. Doubtless, the Department is disappointed that so many schools have insisted on keeping their school community rather than going for determinations from the local SACRE which would cause schools to be split along religious lines. The effect of their new interpretation will be to increase requests for determinations, since the more specific the Christian theological content of collective worship, the more difficult it becomes for pupils from Muslim, Hindu, Jewish and other religious backgrounds to participate, to say nothing of students with genuine secular convictions. The Department insists upon a definition of worship which is drawn, they say, from 'common parlance'. No allowance is made for the educational context of the acts of collective worship. The effect is to turn the school into a worshipping community and the assembly hall into a place of worship. Since participation (and not merely presence) is required of all pupils, the effect is that being registered on the school roll becomes an act of religious commitment. In all sorts of ways, too many to be detailed here, the freedom which the law offers to headteachers, parents and pupils is being denied by the Department's interpretation.

The educational objections

The DfE believes that the way to raise standards in religious education is to improve the agreed syllabuses. This policy, however, is not grounded on evidence. Not only is the Department characteristically ungenerous in its approval of the recent agreed syllabuses, many of which are excellent, but it fails to notice that there is little or no evidence linking effective classroom teaching with the quality of the local agreed syllabus. If the standards of teaching religious education are not as good as they should be, the reason lies in the fact that huge numbers of teachers have never had any training in the subject, especially in the primary school, and that even in the secondary school a large proportion of RE teachers have no qualifications in their subject. Provisions for in-service training are weak and growing steadily weaker as a direct consequence of government policy. In addition, timetable provision is seldom adequate and the funds available to spend on RE resources are usually pitifully low. These aspects are not given due weight in the draft circular.

Not only is the department mistaken in believing that the basic problem lies in the agreed syllabuses, but what it offers by way of improving these syllabuses is little more than insisting on driving a wedge between Christianity and the other principal religions. The two halves of the famous 1988 sentence, in section 8(3), which could be thought of as a general description of a syllabus, if common parlance was heeded, are now used to separate one from the other. Indeed, the view which the DfE has of British society is that it is to be seen mainly as divided between Christian and what they consistently call non-Christian or other religions. When the Department speaks of raising standards, what it means is that Christian shall be separated from non-

Christian, both in the classroom and in collective worship. The separation applies both to content and to people. This is all the government has to offer by way of enabling religious education to make a contribution to the spiritual and moral development of the school and the community.

The theology of the DfE

If one examines the speeches made in Parliament, the range of departmental letters and other correspondence, together with the draft circular and various leaflets and speeches, it is possible to extract the outlines of what has now become a government theology. This centres upon three key concepts which occur again and again in the rhetoric.

The first concept is that of integrity. The integrity of Christianity and the other religions is to be preserved. Integrity means purity, being intact, not being mixed or adulterated. It means that religions are to be taught and practised in watertight compartments. Having insisted on this, the next step is to argue that children cannot be expected to study more than two religions, or three at the most. Since the DfE believes that Christianity should always be one of these, it follows that several of the remaining principle religions are bound to be marginalized. The next step is to claim that the requirements of the law at a given key stage could be met by teaching only one religion. Thus, the integrity of Christianity leads into the monopoly of Christianity. In spite of the disarming way in which all religions are said to have their integrity, we find that integrity means purity and purity means separation and separation means predomination.

This leads us to the second favourite expression used to describe Christianity: Christianity must be predominant. This promotes a competitive relationship between religions. As the other faiths become aware of Christian expansionist ambitions they in turn become more strident. We even talk about such things as 'percentage market shares'.

The insistence upon Christian predomination creates a majority and a minority, powerful and powerless groups. This finds a parallel in the third characteristic conception of Christianity as understood by the government: Christianity is to be regarded as the heritage of this country. The government shows no interest in Christianity as a worldwide faith, nor in the Christian heritage of other countries. Moreover, it becomes perfectly clear that Muslim and Jewish children are not to regard themselves as part of this country's heritage, since this is confined to the Christian heritage. They are only represented here. We must divide religions and believers into the heritage religion and the represented religion.

Christianity as the ideology of purity, power and nationhood

The government theology presents Christianity as the binding ideology of purity and power which will be the basis of nationhood, the purely powerful nation, the purity of national power, the power of national purity. But this is no basis for nation building. The United Kingdom belongs to all its people. Every man, woman and child, whatever his or her religion, is part of this country's ongoing heritage.

The concepts of integrity and predomination are seriously flawed as descriptions of the Christian faith. There is a view of Christianity which says of the pagan centurion, 'For he loves our nation, and he built us our synagogue' (Luke 7:5). There is another view of Christianity which cries out, 'They will come from east and west, and from north and south, and will eat in the Kingdom of God' (Luke 13:29). There is one Christianity which says that the fundamental distinction between people is whether they are Christian or non-Christian. There is another Christian faith which declares that the fundamental distinction is between the rich and the poor, between those who recognize Christ in the prisoner and the homeless and those who do not. There is one Christianity which says that barriers, whether economic, social or ethnic, must be erected in order to control access into the presence of God. There is another which turns over the tables of the money-changers and cries out that 'my house shall be called a house of prayer for all the nations' (Mark 11:17).

The Role of the Religious Groups on SACREs

Autumn 1993

Everyone with an interest in religious education knows that since 1988 every Local Education Authority is required to establish a Standing Advisory Council on Religious Education, and that in England these bodies are made up of four representative groups, while in Wales each SACRE has three groups only. The principle behind this arrangement is that there are three interested parties in religious education: the teachers, the religions and the community. In Wales, where there is no established church, this threefold character is plain; in England the religions are represented by two groups, since the Church of England has a group of its own.

The role of the group representing the community seems clear enough. The Local Education Authority is responsible for authorizing an agreed syllabus. As long as this local responsibility for religious education remains, it is appropriate that the elected and co-opted representatives of the community should be present at the advisory stage (the SACRE), the syllabus-making stage (the Agreed Syllabus Conference) and the final stage of adoption and authorization (the LEA). The role of the teachers' group is equally clear. Those who are to teach the syllabus have an important part to play in creating it and in advising the LEA about it.

The role of the religious group is, however, less clear. If we take a production model, we might say that the religions are there as the raw material from which the product (the agreed syllabus) is assembled. This model offers a view of the role of the religious groups which is too passive. It is to be hoped that the individual members of the religious groups will be truly religious people, and to that extent they will indeed be examples of that which is to be studied. Nevertheless, they are not there because they are religious but because they are representatives of their religious communities. The teachers, when looking for examples of model religious believers to meet their children, might or might not invite someone from the SACRE. Is it then the actual religious communities which are the objects of study, and do their representatives on the SACRE have a sort of exemplary status? Again, one must hope that this is true of SACRE members, but it remains the case that the role of the religious communities cannot be confined to this passive function. They are not there only to meet the needs of a phenomenological approach to the curriculum. Moreover, this approach would not make sense of the Church of England group, since the phenomenological needs of religious education could just as well be satisfied by the Welsh model, in which all the religious representatives were available conveniently for study in one group.

Persisting with the market model, we might say that the religious groups represent the shareholders while the teachers are the sales force and the children are the consumers. The religious groups are thus thought of as the beneficiaries, those who have a stake in the success of the enterprise. They are separate from the LEA group because the industry is not fully nationalized. It exists as a mixed economy, where the agents of government contract with private enterprise. On this model, the Church of England group would occupy an in-between position, as a sort of government quango, which would account for its particular structure in England.

An extension of the 'raw material' model, what we have called the 'object of study' approach, would be to say that the religions are represented on SACREs in order to exercise a consultative role about their own contribution to the curriculum. They are not exactly the object of study, but are the guarantors of accuracy. They would thus have a sort of normative role, contributing the quality of the content which was to be presented. No doubt this is a significant aspect of their role but it has its limits. These become clear if we consider some possible analogies. Let us suppose that we had advisory councils for the teaching of modern languages. Such bodies would surely contain people who spoke the relevant languages, but it is equally certain that they would not be on the council just because they spoke the relevant language, but because they had some expertise of an educational or academic kind. One would not just assemble a lot of people who spoke French; one would gather people experienced in teaching French, or specialists in the study of some aspect of French language or culture. You might ask the local French community to send a representative, but in the teaching of modern languages it does not seem to work this way with or without a local council. Such an approach would whittle away the difference between the teachers' group on the SACRE and the group or groups representing the religious communities. While the religious communities often send as their representatives people who do have special skills in the study or the communication of religion, this is not required of them. All that is required is that they should be a representative.

There seems to have been an evolution in the conception of the religious groups or committees since they began in the 1920s and 30s. Agreed Syllabus Conferences before 1944 were largely composed of people who were not there just because they were representatives of the communities, but because they had some special theological or educational contribution to make. Thus the conference often contained professors of theology from nearby universities, or scholarly priests and ministers. The situation was closer to the imaginary modern languages analogy. Over the years the emphasis upon community participation and representation seems to have increased. No doubt this tells us something about the growth of multi-faith Britain, with the growing self-consciousness of the various religious communities, together with the increased sense of parental responsibility for schools.

We see then that the consultative model has its limitations. Moreover, one could obtain advice from the communities without constituting them as a special group on SACREs, in the way undertaken by the National Curriculum Council in its 1993 consultations with representatives of the various religions in creating a 1993 syllabus model. Also the consultative model in which the religious groups gave advice on how they themselves should be presented would still leave the Church of England group in an anomalous position. It is against the law for religious education to be presented in a denominational way, and the Church of England is at least a denomination.

Certainly, some study of the Church of England in English religious education would not be inappropriate, but this hardly requires a separate group on the SACRE. We come back therefore to the second suggestion made above. The religious groups are there not only in a 'study of religion' role and not only in a role as curriculum consultants, but as managers. They have a proprietorial role to play. It is in the exercising of this function that the religious groups encounter their most delicate responsibilities.

Religious communities and curriculum management

The temptations of management are many, and it would be too idealistic to pretend that representatives of religious communities are immune from them. The representative role itself appears to legitimate a concern for the interests of the community so represented. Thus, a naive view of the role of the religious representative would be to see it as guaranteeing the rights and privileges of the community or the religious faith on the curriculum. This is described as a naive position because what is being managed here is an experience of learning within a context of agreement. We must never stop emphasizing that what is being managed is not religious or devotional life, or local community politics but religious education in schools and that this is done through an agreed syllabus. The management of learning is not only a subtle problem of human relationships within institutional contexts, but in the SACRE context it cannot be confined to the management of that learning which concerns the interests of the community being represented. To put it more bluntly, Anglicans are not on SACREs to advise on Anglican learning or even on Christian learning, just as Muslims are not in the 'other denominations' group to advise on Muslim learning. This is not to deny (under the consultancy model which we have discussed) that they have a role in this respect; it is to assert that the role must not be naively and narrowly conceived in this way alone. Muslims are

129

present on the SACRE as members of a very significant religious community who thus are called to a role in the management of religious education as a whole. This, and only this, can justify a separate Church of England group. If the Church of England begins to conceive of its role as managing the curriculum in the interests of Christianity alone, or as offering consultancy in Christianity alone, the case for a group representing the established church is lost.

Another temptation of the managerial role is to imagine that the religious communities are intended to be the principal beneficiaries – the shareholder model. The problem with this conception is that it does not provide an adequate rationale for religious education supported by the general taxpayer in schools which are available for the education of all children, whether religious or not. Religious education is not only for children from religious families; it is a contribution to the education of all children. The agreed syllabus of religious education does not exist in order to advance the interests of the religious communities but as a contribution to the moral and spiritual development of the entire community and of the nation. Muslims are not called there to protect or advance the interests of Muslims but to care for the education of everyone. The same is true of the representatives of the Sikh and Jewish communities and so on. Of course, this overall view is a special responsibility of the LEA group, but it is important to emphasize that an overall view must be taken by every group on the SACRE. Representation on SACRE implies a general educational responsibility. The SACRE is not there to advise on religious schools but on ordinary schools. SACREs thus rest upon the assumption that every religious representative will think and feel beyond the limits of his or her own religious faith. The implications of SACRE are ecumenical and dialogical. No member of SACRE can distinguish between *our* children and *your* children. All children are *our* children because we are the community and this is *our* religious education.

The role of the religious groups and the agreed syllabus legislation

In discussing the present tendency for the representatives of the community to interpret their role in somewhat narrow community lines, a number of factors were mentioned including the increasingly multicultural character of Britain in recent decades. It must also be pointed out that the tendency towards community competition and religious rivalry has regrettably been fostered by the famous clause 8(3) of the 1988 Education Reform Act, which requires new agreed syllabuses 'to reflect the fact that the principal religious traditions in Great Britain are in the main Christian whilst taking account of the teaching and practices of the other principal religious represented in Great Britain'. At its best, this expression could be interpreted in a broad way, leading to an ecumenical spirit and a dialogical approach. However, it is equally possible to interpret the words in a spirit of competition which encourages religious aggrandisement on the part of the powerful and a responding defensive aggression on the part of the less powerful religious communities. It is most unfortunate that the wording of 8(3) could be taken to suggest that the religious syllabus will consist of the study of religions, one by one, which places the religions in a context of immediate comparison and competition. It is out of this context that the recent and present sterile debates about so-called balance in the curriculum have sprung.

The role of the Church of England

This is a good moment in the history of education to return to tradition. In 1830 Samuel Taylor Coleridge described the educational responsibility of the Church of England as going beyond the interests of the Christian Church, in a strictly religious and confessional sense, to include the whole character and purpose of national education 'in producing and reproducing, in preserving, continuing and effecting the necessary sources and conditions of national civilization.... The proper object and end of the national church is civilization with freedom' (Samuel Taylor Coleridge, *On the Constitution of the Church and the State*, 1830, London, Routledge & Kegan Paul). In order to do this, the national church in its teaching office is to spread abroad all that knowledge which advances our common humanity, builds up men and women into the freedom and moral responsibility without which citizenship, and thus the state itself, is impossible. This is the interest of the state in possessing a national church, and in conferring upon it educational responsibilities. The fact that the religion embodied in the national church is Christianity is, according to Coleridge, a 'blessed accident'. Christianity is the aid and instrument by which the national church pursues its purposes. It is thus a means to build up the common good.

If we apply Coleridge's religious philosophy of education to the responsibilities of the national church today we might well conclude that national education, as undergirded by the moral and spiritual traditions of humanity, is to be fostered by men and women of good will from all religious traditions, amongst whom Christians have a special place but not a unique responsibility. This is why the Church of England, as representing the national church, has a special committee or group on the Agreed Syllabus Conference and the SACRE. If in pursuing its purposes, the national church becomes a vehicle for the expansion of Christianity in competition with other faiths and no longer a vehicle for the promotion of the spirituality and freedom which is the basis of our humanity, then the case for the Church having its own committee becomes weaker. Rather, through its own committee the national church should lead the way in promoting an ecumenical and a humanitarian vision and thus becoming a model which could be safely followed by all the represented religions.

The national association of SACREs

In the context of a reflection upon the national church and its role in promoting the national culture, it is significant that the majority of SACREs have now formed themselves into a National Association. The newly formed National Association should do much to strengthen both the local and the national aspects of the role of religious education in building up the moral and spiritual culture of the country. In that sense, the National Association and each of its individual SACREs may be looked upon as an expression of the national church in its teaching office in the sense used by Coleridge. The heart of the enterprise should be the group which particularly represents the national church. This conception, however, depends upon a non-sectarian view of the Church of England.

School Worship and the 1988 Education Reform Act

Summer 1989

A good deal of the following article was included in my 1989 booklet The Act Unpacked: The Meaning of the Religious Education Clauses of the 1988 Education Reform Act for Religious Education *(Derby, CEM)*.

Unfortunately, the then Conservative Government did not commend the broad and tolerant interpretation of the Act which my article advocated, but went for a much stricter theological definition of collective worship. This was published in the Department for Education Circular 1/94. One theological definition leads to another, and in my Royal Society of Arts Lecture 'Worship: The Search for Spirituality' *(published in* Future Progress in Religious Education (The Templeton London Lectures at the RSA), *London, RSA, 1995, pp. 27–38) I traced the development of these theological definitions, showing their increasing absurdity and futility.*

The most important feature of the new Act as far as religion is concerned is the fact that for the first time Christianity is specifically mentioned. Fears were expressed about this inclusion, and recent events have tended to confirm these, at least as far as school worship is concerned. The situation regarding the content of the classroom religious education is not so serious, since the effect of the legislation should be to strengthen a multi-faith approach. The situation with school worship is more delicate, the sections of the Act which deal with it are complex, and the consequences for the life of the school and its surrounding communities are more immediate.

It was early in May of 1988 that rumours of a proposed change in the school worship law began to circulate. Little time or opportunity was provided for reasonable professional consultation, and since the affair was proceeding through amendments tabled in the House of Lords little could be done but write letters, make urgent telephone calls, and watch developments week by week. During these months I wrote again and again to the government, to Members of Parliament in both Houses, to the bishops and archbishops of the Church of England and to other bodies who appeared to be prominent in such negotiations as were said to be taking place, but all to little effect. The schools are now faced with the problem of interpreting what is undoubtedly the most obscure and complicated piece of religious education legislation in the history of this country, and the confusion and misunderstanding which has been created is no less distressing because it was all so predictable.

Making the best of it

Fortunately, when we come to examine the actual words of the Act we find a situation which is more ambiguous than the propaganda which surrounded its passage through Parliament, and offers a greater range of options to schools than might have been expected. Perhaps there was a conflict between the rather crude aspirations of some of those who argued most strongly for Christian school worship and those political and professional circles where the Act was finally drafted. That may well become a question for future research. Our present responsibility as teachers and as citizens is to study the Act carefully, and to interpret it wisely and responsibly in the interests of our schools and the communities they serve.

'Wholly or mainly of a broadly'

The crucial words defining school worship are to be found in section 7(1). Collective worship 'shall be wholly or mainly of a broadly Christian character'. The following sub-section tells us that 'collective worship is of a broadly Christian character if it reflects the broad traditions of Christian belief without being distinctive of any particular Christian denomination'.

It should be pointed out first of all that the expression 'Christian worship' does not appear in sections 6 or 7, where the internal arrangements for collective worship are described. It is only when we come to section 12 where the administrative arrangements external to the school are described that we read of 'Christian collective worship'. 'Christian worship' is perhaps a convenient summary expression, but in legislation as complex as this summaries can be misleading. The wording of the Act makes it clear that what is envisaged in schools is no simple, straightforward act of Christian worship. There are thousands upon thousands of Christian denominations, and almost all actual Christian worship takes place in these and is obviously distinctive of one or the other denominations. It might be thought, perhaps, that the acts of worship envisaged here might be of an ecumenical character, but this would be an over-hasty conclusion. The Act does not speak of school worship as being inter-denominational or ecumenical, nor indeed is it even to be modelled upon traditional Christian worship of any kind. It is significant that school worship is to reflect 'the broad traditions of Christian *belief*' not those of Christian worship. Why is the word 'belief' used at this point rather than the word 'worship'?

Moreover, the Act does not speak of school worship as being 'characteristically Christian', 'uniquely Christian', 'definitely Christian' or any such expression but, rather, as being 'broadly Christian'. So general is this term that some sort of definition was apparently felt to be necessary, but the definition in section 7(3) is itself remarkably broad and general. All that is necessary to constitute a broadly Christian act of worship is that the broad traditions (note the plural) of Christian belief shall be reflected. We are not told that these traditions of Christian belief shall be affirmed, presented, acknowledged, proclaimed, made the basis of the worship or any other of the dozens of similar expressions which might with clarity have been used. School worship is merely to *reflect* them. This is a curiously distant and muted expression, and one must interpret it in the context of the schools themselves, the range and variety of pupils in them, and the educational constraints to be exercised.

'The broad traditions of Christian belief'

What are these broad traditions of Christian belief that are to be reflected in school assembly? It has already been pointed out that it is Christian belief not Christian worship which is to be reflected, but what is this? At first sight one might suppose that Orthodoxy, Protestantism and Roman Catholicism would be the main traditions of Christian belief. This, however, would be too simple. School worship is not to be denominational and Roman Catholicism, at least, is a denomination.

Moreover, we are encouraged to think of the Christian tradition as plural. There is no reference to a single tradition but to several. Presumably belief in God is one of these, and so an act of school worship meets the conditions of this section if it reflects belief in God. Belief in Jesus Christ as the Son of God, and in the Trinity would also be amongst the broad traditions of Christian belief, and it would be perfectly appropriate for acts of school worship to reflect these as well, but one must remember that there is no suggestion that school worship should reflect *all* the broad traditions of Christian belief, or should concentrate upon those which are distinctive or unique. When we realize that even the ways and the extent to which this already very general description is to be worked out in schools (if at all!) are dependent upon educational considerations which the Act goes on to outline, it becomes still more clear that what is envisaged is something very curious indeed.

In seeking to define school worship more closely, it has become necessary to delineate the educational context in which it takes place. The result is a recognition that collective worship in county schools is not to be compared with anything which goes on in religious communities outside schools. School worship is *sui generis*. Headteacher and governors are here called upon to exercise a creative, educational imagination in providing for the spiritual needs of their pupils, in meetings (collectives not congregations) which shall be a kind of worship but which shall be defined by the school context and not by the context of the Church.

The options in front of the schools are clearly quite wide, but this is not all. School worship is to reflect these broad traditions of Christian belief, and so is to become 'of a broadly Christian character' but this broadly Christian character is not insisted upon. A whole range of qualifications are now introduced, and each of these deserves consideration, since each opens up new possibilities of patterns for school assemblies.

'Wholly or mainly'

Not a single act of school worship has to be *wholly* (as opposed to *mainly*) of this broadly Christian character, not from the start of the school year until its end. Of course, it would be perfectly legal for a school to provide nothing but acts of collective worship which *were* wholly of a broadly Christian character, but the Act does not *require* that a single act of this kind should ever take place. This important point seems to have escaped attention in all the clamour of the publicity which has surrounded the clauses. The fact is that the law offers the school an alternative: 'mainly' is just as good as 'wholly'.

While it would be premature at this stage to go into detail, the Bible surely reflects the broad traditions of Christian belief. If an act of collective worship is composed of six verses from one of the Psalms, with five verses from the Qur'an, together with some simple prayers addressed to God, it would meet the requirements of the Act. (At other times, this proportion could be reversed.) Of course, inasmuch as Islam, Christianity and Judaism all represent the Abrahamic tradition they may be thought of as reflecting each other, and as sharing in the faith of Abraham. In that case, the act of collective worship described here would be not 'mainly' but 'wholly' of a broadly Christian character, as defined by the law. By the same token, it could be thought of as being wholly or mainly of a broadly Islamic character, which is, however, not the concern of the Act. An act of collective worship would still be *mainly* of a broadly Christian character if it contained minority elements from religious traditions which in no way reflect the broad traditions of Christian belief.

'Most such Acts'

That is not all. Nothing in the legislation requires the schools to offer these acts of worship which fall under the heading 'mainly of a broadly Christian' character every day. Section 7(4) specifically declares that it will be sufficient if in any school term *most* of the acts of collective worship are like this. The remainder need not even be of a mainly broadly Christian character.

We are now in a position to begin to create some patterns. It would be possible for a school to offer acts of collective worship which were mainly of a broadly Christian character on Mondays, Wednesday and Fridays. On Tuesdays and Thursdays school worship need not be of a broadly Christian character at all. Nothing is said about what it shall be on those days, apart from the fact that it shall be an act of collective worship, and we may suppose that the more imaginative schools will go on doing what they have been doing for decades, which is creating educational experiences of a broadly spiritual nature in which fundamental beliefs and values are affirmed, meditated upon and celebrated. These school assemblies may well reflect the pluralistic nature of the school community, but so may the ones which are to be mainly of a broadly Christian character, so it may well turn out in the end that there is not much difference. Indeed, it would be extremely difficult to argue that the kinds of school worship which are thought of here as taking place on Tuesdays and Thursdays do not in any case reflect the broad traditions of Christian belief in certain significant and appropriate ways. Any legalistic (how appropriate that word is!) attempt to create clear-cut distinctions between these various kinds of school worship seems futile.

There are, unfortunately, many schools in which there have been no such imaginative patterns of spiritual celebration and affirmation. School assembly has all too often degenerated into a mere formality, often entirely secularized, given over to school administration and moralizing discourses. Religious education teachers have been trying for years to replace these perfunctory and boring school assemblies by more lively spiritual occasions, and we must hope that the 1988 Act will lend strength to this cause.

The educational context of school worship

Again, this is not all. Section 7(4) sets out a new range of possibilities. The Act now distinguishes between *extent* and *ways* in the conduct of school worship. The headteacher and the governors are to consider the extent to which it is appropriate for school worship to reflect the broad traditions of Christian belief, if at all. In addition, they are to consider 'the ways in which those traditions are reflected' in any acts of school worship. We are thus encouraged to think of a variety of ways in which the broad reflection might take place. We need to consider school assemblies as being 'ways of reflection' in relation to the broad traditions of Christian belief, and to prepare models of what these various ways might be. 'Extent' refers mainly to frequency and 'ways' refers to the style or manner of the worship. And what, we may ask, is to guide headteachers and governors in these considerations? Are they to examine the history of Christian liturgy? Are they to read up the manuals of Christian doctrine? Are they to take note of what goes on in the churches nearby? Nothing of the sort.

The heads and governors are to act in their capacity as educators. They are, for the most part, not theologians and, although we may hope that all will have access to expert religious education staff, the decisions about school worship are not to be religious decisions in any obvious or literal sense of the word. This is what we meant when we said that school worship is a class all of its own. There is nothing like it elsewhere.

The educational considerations are specified in section 7(5). First, 'any circumstances relating to the family background of the pupils concerned which are relevant to determining the character of the collective worship which is appropriate in their case' are to be taken into account. It will be relevant here to consider not only whether pupils come from homes where the Christian or some other faith is practised, but whether pupils come from secular homes. Nothing could be more relevant in determining the ways in which school assembly shall be presented than the fact that most of the pupils in our schools have little or no familiarity with religious worship in their home or community life outside the school. The other factors which are to be taken into account are the age and aptitudes of the pupils. Is there an aptitude for worship? Is there an aptitude for religious experience?

These educational considerations are extremely important for the conduct of school worship, since they bring it for the first time into the full light of professional responsibility. Naturally, the best practices of school assembly in the past have always taken account of pupils' ages and there is an extensive literature dealing with the question of school worship for the primary school as distinct from the secondary school and so on. These considerations of human development are now required by law, and are no longer a matter for the unsupported enthusiasm of the individual head or the conscientious religious education department. What should collective worship be for the student aged seventeen and over? What should it be for the infant? One of the broadest traditions of Christian belief is that human personality should be respected, and that love takes precedence over faith. Indeed, it would be difficult to imagine anything more appropriate by way of training for headteachers and governors perplexed about school worship than to read the thirteenth chapter of the first letter of Paul to the Corinthians, the famous poem on love. Of all the traditions of Christian belief, this is the broadest. Let love be our guide, and we shall not go far astray.

The role of the SACRE

That is not all. If, after all these qualifications have been explored, and the educational considerations have been taken fully into account, there still remains a doubt about the appropriateness of whatever a broadly Christian character might mean, there is a way out. The headteacher and the governing body may make application to their local SACRE for relief in whole or in part from the requirement to present any acts of school worship which will reflect in any way at all and to any extent at all even the broadest traditions of Christian belief. It is the responsibility of the SACRE to deal with these applications and to make a 'determination' on the question. An application may be made on behalf of the entire school, or on behalf of any class or description of pupils in the school.

The first thing to be said about such an appeal is that it should be the last resort. It is a matter of great regret that many headteachers and governing bodies seem to have been panicked by the misleading publicity which has surrounded the Education Reform Act into making a premature application to SACRE for a determination. While one cannot but feel sympathy for such schools, especially when containing pupils from various religious traditions, it must be emphasized that if the full scope of school worship permitted by the Act is carefully studied, these appeals may become less frequent. In many cases, a school which finds it necessary to apply for a determination is a school which has found its internal divisions irreconcilable, one in which it is admitted that school worship can no longer play a unifying role in the life of the whole school community.

Nevertheless, realities must be faced. Once a privilege is given to one religious tradition (in this case, Christianity) natural justice demands that similar privileges should be extended to all. Now we begin to realize the wisdom of the Butler Act of 1944 which steadfastly refused to define school worship but left it to the common sense of those immediately responsible in each locality.

Let us, however, go on with our policy of trying to make the best of it. Even these sections of the Act give rise to important principles which should be carefully studied.

The responsibility of the school

First, we must notice that the collective worship which is provided in a school as a result of a determination by SACRE remains the responsibility of the head and the governors. The schools are permitted to make application to opt out of section 7 (wholly or mainly of a broadly) but not section 6 (collective worship). It is the responsibility of the head and the governors to ensure that school worship takes place, whether under section 7 *or* following the determination provided by SACRE. A school may make application to SACRE on

139

behalf of a number of Muslim pupils. That does not mean that the resulting school worship, as determined by SACRE, will be mosque worship. It will continue to be school worship. It does not fall within the power of SACRE to enable mosques, synagogues, temples or any other places of worship to have their own services for their own pupils on school premises. It remains possible, of course, for the parents of any pupil to withdraw that pupil from any collective worship whatever in school. Under certain conditions those pupils could be provided with acts of worship which could really be called mosque worship or whatever. But as long as we are talking about the acts of worship required by section 6 of the Act as determined by SACRE these remain *school* collective worship.

The Act does not specify that the age, aptitude and family backgrounds of pupils are to be taken into account when considering the nature of these SACRE-determined school assemblies, but there is nothing at all which suggests that educational and professional responsibility ceases once SACRE has made a determination.

It must also be remembered that there may be many patterns of determination. We described a situation in which the 'mainly of a broadly' type of worship took place on three days of the week. It would be perfectly in order for a school to make application to SACRE for broadly Hindu worship to take place on these three days, but for the whole school to meet together on the remaining two days of the week. Determination is not an all-or-nothing matter.

School worship is non-denominational

These reflections are supported by the fact that the collective school worship which is determined by SACRE continues to share with the 'wholly or mainly of a broadly' type one important feature: it shall not 'be distinctive of any particular Christian or other religious denomination but this shall not be taken as preventing that worship from being distinctive of any particular faith'. It is worth repeating the point made above about the characteristics of actual religious worship: it always or nearly always takes place in denominational form. Jewish worship, for example, is usually either orthodox or liberal or reformed. The school worship determined by SACRE can only be typical of a faith as a whole. This underlines the fact that school worship is *sui generis*.

It is curious that we should be told at this point – section 7(6.b) – that school worship determined by SACRE shall not be distinctive of any particular *Christian* denomination but shall be distinctive of the Christian faith. This helps us to see clearly the difference between the normal school worship, whether it be 'wholly or mainly of a broadly Christian character' or not and that *different* kind of school worship which is to be 'distinctive' of the Christian faith, the kind which is only available to a school when it has successfully made application for this type of collective worship to SACRE. If there is one single misunderstanding which has confused the issue it has been the failure to distinguish the 'wholly or mainly of a broadly' type from the 'distinctive' type. Everyone seems to think that the section 7 type of school worship is to be distinctively Christian. This is not true. Worship which is distinctive of the Christian faith is available only to schools who apply successfully to SACRE for a determination in this respect, and it is clear that SACRE should exercise the greatest caution in permitting any county school to deviate from the 'wholly or mainly of a broadly' type in favour of something more distinctively Christian. If they are sufficiently distinctively Christian themselves, these pupils should be getting their distinctive Christian worship in their churches and their homes, and should be content to take part in the collective life of the whole school, seeking common ground in peace, hope and love. As always, determination should be a last resort.

Nurturing the multi-faith school

We have remarked that in some cases a school which makes application to its SACRE for a determination might be a school which had failed to reconcile its internal communities. On the other hand, this might not be the case, and every school will obviously do all it can to ensure that it remains a harmonious community. Even when it has been found necessary as a last resort to seek a determination from SACRE for some acts of collective worship to be distinctive of a religious faith, we may still hope that the result will be a school which cares for and encourages the spirituality of all its pupils. We envisage schools in which all the pupils meet together for mutual exploration of their various religious traditions in their common religious education classes under the guidance of world religions agreed syllabuses. During school worship they sometimes meet together for affirmation, celebration and meditation on common beliefs and values, or for dialogue on each other's faiths, while at other times pupils will deepen their insight into their own religious traditions by exploring the worshipful characteristics proper to each tradition. There is no reason why a rhythm should not be established which will include both coming together and drawing apart. If supervised with wisdom, there seems no reason why schools of this kind should not nurture spiritual life at least as successfully as they have done in the past, and perhaps more so.

What stands in the way of this is not so much the Act itself, but the tribalistic and protective emotions which have been aroused by a partisan

Christian belief. It is now up to all of us in education to ensure that a responsible practice based upon a genuine understanding of the Act prevails over sectarian strife.

When we say that the Act does not stand in the way of spiritual nurture we mean that (contrary to the popular view) it does not support a Christian monopoly which leaves no room for other forms of spirituality. On the other hand, there remains a sense in which the Act certainly does stand in the way. The complexities of trying to legislate so as to require some sort of specific faith commitment in educational worship have produced something which may well be self-defeating. The danger is that busy people will go for simple solutions. It was the Butler Act which offered the best simple solution but the Baker Act has rejected this. The other kinds of simple solution, those which the tribalistic religious groups tend to support, will breed disaster for the common life of our schools. Although as good citizens and responsible educators we shall continue to try to make the best of it, it is possible that collective worship under the 1988 Act will be unworkable.

Religious Worship and School Worship

Spring 1990

I had already emphasized the educational character of the collective worship required by the 1988 Education Reform Act in my booklet The Act Unpacked, *published about a year before this particular editorial. It is to be found under the heading* 'Educationally Appropriate Worship' *on pp. 19–21 of the booklet. In the article which follows, the educational context of collective worship is examined in some detail.*

One of the most striking features of the 1988 legislation on collective worship is that the religious content and the educational context have both been emphasized. This double emphasis is leading to a new understanding of collective worship, which springs out of a contrast between religious worship and school worship.

The emphasis upon the Christian character of school worship

The religious nature of the school assembly has been underlined in the 1988 Act by requiring that it shall usually be of a broadly Christian character. In the 1944 Act school worship was only defined negatively. It was not to be distinctive of any particular denomination. Nothing was said of a positive nature about what it should be. The new legislation retains the prohibition against denominationalism and adds a positive requirement. School worship is to reflect the general character of one religion in particular, i.e. Christianity. We may thus say that the specifically religious nature of school worship has been heightened.

The moment this is done, however, certain consequences appear. In the social and educational conditions of contemporary Britain it is not possible to heighten the specifically religious character of one of our public institutions without at the same time introducing qualifications. So it is that the 1988 Act both builds up and tears down simultaneously; it defines and it redefines. The Act giveth and the Act taketh away. Blessed be this feature of the Act, because without it the required school worship would be so inappropriate as to be unworkable.

The Act takes away the Christian emphasis which it has been given, partly by qualifying it and partly by emphasizing its educational significance. School worship is not to be Christian worship pure and simple. It is not to be distinctively Christian or uniquely Christian but merely to reflect a broad Christian character. It does not even have to have, possess, exhibit or demonstrate this character but only to reflect it. Moreover, this broad character need only be reflected mainly and not wholly. Even this need only occur on most of the days of the school term. Thus, if we suppose a twelve-week term consisting of sixty days, twenty-nine of these days need not reflect a trace of even the most general Christian character whatever. It is even more remarkable that the criterion for judging whether or not collective worship is of a broadly Christian character does not refer to Christian worship but to Christian belief. What has gone on in Christian worship down the ages is not relevant to a consideration of whether or not school worship reflects a broadly Christian character, since the determination of this character lies in whether or not it reflects the broad traditions of Christian belief. There is no easy way of knowing what these might be, but we would not be justified in assuming that Christian doctrine was intended. It is significant that the Act does not speak of the main Christian beliefs (plural) but of the broad traditions of Christian belief (singular). This could reasonably refer to the ways of Christian believing, such as the way of meditation, the way of practical good works, the way of community life or the intellectual and spiritual paths. Be that as it may, it is clear that the definitions which are offered in the Act are far from clear. This is as it should be since without this now-you-see-it/now-you-don't quality, the Act would make even less sense.

However vaguely and indirectly, it remains the case that we now have an Act of Parliament which prescribes Christian belief as a norm for something which is to take place at least partially and rather frequently in our schools. This has to be recognized as the introduction of a confessional element into educational practice, something which Parliament has studiously avoided in all previous educational legislation.

The new confessionalism

The ambiguous quality of this confessionalism is apparent in the Act itself, and this must be reflected in our appraisal of it. If we think of it positively, we may appreciate the fact that the British people still possess some religious traditions, however enfeebled. The sociologist Peter Berger has used the expression 'the homeless mind' as the title of one of his studies of contemporary society. This refers to the rootlessness, the vacuum of values, the death of unifying and meaning-giving symbols which seems to be such a feature of modernity. Up to a point, we should be grateful that in the midst of our destruction of the environment and the resurgence of market values there remains a spiritual heart which still faintly beats.

Whether we can appreciate the Act in this positive way depends to some extent upon our estimation of what the lawyers would call the mischief which the Act was intended to overcome. If the mischief was the general secularization of society, as reflected in the collapse of school assembly in many schools and its trivialization and perfunctory nature in others, then we may respond rather warmly to this insistence that school life must not be permitted to lose sight of spiritual values. If, however, the mischief lay rather in a fear of alternative spiritualities, then our appreciation will be more guarded. The horror which motivated at least some of the speakers in the Parliamentary debates appears to have been not so much secularization but the presence of great world faiths other than Christianity. There seems to have been a shrinking from syncretism, a fear of contamination leading to loss of purity. It is this primitive fear of the largely unknown and foreign, this defensive identity, which lies behind the frequently repeated allegation that school worship before the 1988 Act was becoming a mish-mash. Since British religious education has been wholly committed to a world religions approach for many years, any interpretation of the religious clauses of the new Act which saw it as a protest movement against world religions would lead to a rather worrying split between the ideals of the teaching profession and those of the Act of Parliament which legislates for it.

The question of what mischief the Act was intended to overcome is an important clue for the interpretation of the significance of the legislation, but this cannot be pursued in detail here. The main point is that whatever the mischief, whether real or imagined, the legislative response was to introduce Christian confessionalism into the schools. This immediately creates important new problems of an educational and social kind and this is why the Act has to quickly undo what it has done.

The educational nature of school worship

There are a number of features which mark out school worship as being quite different from religious worship. The first of these is the frequent and consistent use of the adjective 'collective'. This word is not new. It was already used to describe school worship in the 1944 Act. In the 1988 Act, however, it seems to receive a new emphasis. Perhaps it is in reaction to the heightened confessionalism that the collectivity of school worship is now receiving more attention. A corporate act of worship would be one which involved a body of believers. It would take place on the assumption of unanimity, of a shared faith, a common commitment. The clearest example of this within Christianity is the Communion service, where the believers 'are all of one body' since they all share in the one bread. Collective worship, on the other hand, does not presuppose a common faith. It is the coming together or the collecting of a number of individuals, with various backgrounds and beliefs. It is precisely not common worship but collective worship.

This gives rise to the question: In what sense can a varied group of people as opposed to a unified body engage in an act of worship together? The answer is to be found in the educational context. Collective acts of worship do not occur in the religious communities outside the school. If we are looking for a model for collective school worship, we will not find it in the religious communities. This is a striking fact, but close examination of the Act confirms it.

Collective worship within education structures

Let us examine some of the aspects of the new legislation which places collective worship clearly within the educational context. First, we notice that all pupils in attendance at a maintained school shall take part each day in an act of collective worship on the grounds of their faith. This is no 'gathered' community, in the sense familiar to the churches of the reformed tradition where the believing congregation is gathered out of the world. This aspect has been emphasized by making it clear that the requirement extends beyond the age of compulsory school attendance. It does not matter how old a pupil is; what matters is that the pupil is registered as attending the school. The question of age is to be taken into account in determining the nature of the collective worship, but is not a factor in determining whether or not a pupil shall attend. Collective worship is thus not conceived of as something that you grow out of; it is not something offered to help the development of the younger pupils; it is a formal requirement of institutional membership.

The implications of this participation in the educational institution are developed by insisting that the acts of collective worship shall normally take place 'on the school premises' (section 6(4)). There may be a church, chapel, synagogue or mosque right next door to the school, but it cannot be used for collective worship except on rare and specified occasions. The school premises are themselves an essential context for defining the nature of the collective worship which goes on. To put this worship in a religious building, a building set aside for religious worship, would fundamentally change the nature of the assembly. This is further emphasized by sub-section (4) which states that even when for a 'special occasion' a religious building is used, this shall in no way alter the general principle that normally the school itself shall be used.

No doubt an additional reason for this prohibition of regular use of religious buildings is that almost all places of religious worship are denominational. There are few if any Christian churches; churches are Methodist, or Roman Catholic, and so on. Even if a free evangelical congregation were to insist upon describing itself as nothing but a Christian church, that would not affect the denominational character of its worship.

There are churches dedicated to multi-denominational use and to ecumenism, but there is no suggestion in the Act that collective school worship is to be ecumenical. It is to avoid being distinctive of a denomination not by being ecumenical but by being educational.

Section 6 of the Act makes it clear that collective worship may take place in a range of pupils' groups. Sub-section (7) defines 'school group' as 'any group in which pupils are taught or take part in other school activities'. This is a significant clause for understanding collective school worship. Pupils are not to be drawn together for collective worship on any basis other than the normal arrangements of everyday school life. Usually, that will mean a group in which pupils are taught. Quite so. Teaching and learning is the function of the school, and it is in the places and with the persons with whom pupils learn and are taught that school collective worship is also to take place. If the group which gathers for collective worship is not a teaching group, then it must be a group which has some regular, normal function in 'other school activities'. The wording does not refer to other *religious* activities but to other *school* activities.

Let us suppose that a group of ten or a dozen GCSE students were all Sikhs. It would be possible for the group to meet together for collective worship, not because they happened to be Sikhs but because they were organized into a regular learning activity. A majority of the acts of collective worship in each term would have to reflect the broad traditions of Christian belief, and this would hardly be appropriate for a group of Sikh students. Therefore a determination would have to be sought from the local SACRE, and if that were successful the students could then meet together as Sikhs regardless of whether they were in a GCSE group or not.

Additional educational considerations

Sub-section (4) of section 7 introduces a further range of educational considerations. So far we have seen that headteachers and governors have considerable freedom in determining the type of collective worship which will be appropriate for their school. School assembly may be either wholly or mainly of a certain character, and this character may be present in all assemblies or merely in most assemblies during a given term. What factors are to guide heads and governors in deciding these matters? School assemblies may reflect the broad traditions of Christian belief to various extents. The reflection may be quite intense or it may be rather faint and dim. Moreover, not only the intensity of the reflection but also the ways in which the collective worship actually goes about securing that reflection are under consideration. Not only are there many traditions of Christian belief and several intensities of reflecting them, but they may be reflected in various ways.

This is just about as far as it could be from imposing a set of uniform procedures upon schools. It bears little or no resemblance to a liturgical imposition. We are told that heads and governing bodies may respond to these questions by asking about the appropriate 'character' of the assembly in the light of 'relevant considerations'. Sub-section (5) leaves us in no doubt as to what these considerations are. They make no reference to normal patterns of Christian worship, what goes on in churches, the kind of characteristics of Christian faith which the headteacher and governors themselves may possess and so on. Nothing is said here about definitions of worship one way or another. On the contrary, attention is to be focused entirely upon the characteristics of the children. These acts of collective worship are not to be liturgically-centred but child-centred.

For example, 'any circumstances relating to the family background of the pupils concerned which are relevant to determining the character of the collective worship which is appropriate in their case' must be considered. We are not told what kind of factor might be relevant. Nothing is said to suggest that the relevant factors should be confined to religious questions, however. We are specifically told *'any* circumstances ...'. If the family background of a pupil is entirely secular, that is just as relevant to a consideration of what kind of collective worship might be appropriate as the circumstance when the family background is highly religious. We are not told to consider the religious characteristics of the family background of the pupils, but merely any relevant circumstances of their family backgrounds. If pupils have no contact whatever with religious worship that is just as relevant a consideration as the fact that they have a great deal of contact with a particular religious tradition.

A religious group when meeting together for its characteristic worship can quite legitimately say to any visitor, 'Come and see what we do. We have our own way of doing things. You must fit in with us.' No school can take this line. School collective worship does not have its own way of doing things into which pupils must fit; rather, whatever is done is to be adapted to the nature of the pupils' experiences and needs. It would be quite wrong to impose a certain conception or pattern of collective worship upon pupils for the sake of some supposed definition of religious worship. It is the pupils themselves who are to be the controlling factors in shaping the freedom of the school. This is further strengthened by the reference to the 'ages and aptitudes' of the pupils. Collective worship in schools is not to be instruction into worship but is to be an aspect of religious education. If pupils are to learn from acts of collective worship this learning must be adapted to the characteristics of the learner. If pupils are to participate in collective worship, their ages, aptitudes and family backgrounds must be respected.

Collective worship which is distinctive of a particular faith

Do these educational considerations apply to those acts of collective worship which take place following a determination by SACRE? Sub-section (6) makes it clear that these assemblies must not be distinctive of a denomination. This is consistent with the general tendency to avoid getting entangled in the actual, concrete commitments of religious life outside the school. Nevertheless, the section continues by saying that 'this shall not be taken as preventing that worship from being distinctive of any particular faith'.

These assemblies continue, however, to be acts of *collective* worship. They do not become corporate worship just because they may be distinctive of a particular faith. The headteacher and the governors are still responsible for the general conduct of these determined acts of collective worship, and parents may still withdraw their children from them. They are still to take place on the school premises. We may conclude that even when these assemblies are to be distinctive of a faith that does not mean that they cease to be distinctive of the school context.

What is school worship?

School worship is educational worship. It is an act of worship in which pupils are to learn by and through their participation. The participants never lose their status as pupils or students. They always remain learners. They are never to be treated principally as believers although the fact that they are or are not believers is certainly relevant to the type of educational worship which will be provided. Nevertheless, their status as believers is always and only relevant to their needs as learners, and never the reverse. Collective worship is to be part of their educational experience and not necessarily a part of their religious experience. If there is some sense in which what is provided in collective worship may be thought of as religious experience, then this also is to be appropriated by the students in their capacity as students, i.e. it continues to be part of their educational experience. Whereas in normal religious worship the elements of adoration and praise or whatever are central and any learning which may result is secondary, in school collective worship the reverse is the case. Learning outcomes are primary, and elements of adoration or praise if they exist at all are present in order to enable successful and appropriate educational experiences.

Collective worship and the spiritual

It is true that in the opening section of the Act reference is made to religious education and *religious* worship. The reference here is not to collective worship.

Once again, the context is significant. The responsible educational authorities are to make religious education, religious worship and the National Curriculum available to pupils in such a way as to fulfil the requirements of the following section. In clause 1(2) which follows we are told that this is to be done through providing a 'balanced and broadly-based curriculum which promotes the spiritual, moral' and other aspects of the pupil and of society. Religious worship is thus immediately placed within this purpose. It is thought of as one of the major ways in which the spiritual is to be promoted. Collective worship must not carry the full weight of this, since the curriculum as a whole must also promote the spiritual. It is in this context, however, that the educational nature of collective worship is to be understood.

The principal educational responsibility of school assembly is to promote the spiritual and thus to fulfil one of the principal aims of education. It is as religious worship enters into the administrative details of educational provision that its collectivity emerges. Collective worship is the educational transformation of religious worship.

Collective Worship and the Search for the Spiritual

Spring 1995

A *more detailed form of this article was published as* 'Collective Worship: The search for Spirituality' *in* Future progress in Religious Education, *a series of three lectures sponsored by the John Templeton Foundation in association with the RSA (London, RSA, 1995, pp. 27–38), with supporting responses from Umar Hegedus and Laurie Rosenberg (pp. 38–40).*

Education in Britain has always placed a significant emphasis upon spirituality. In view of the close relation between religion and spirituality in the nineteenth century, it is not surprising that the search for the spiritual should have focused upon worship. As a result of the work of artists and poets, philosophers and theologians, our understanding of the nature of the spiritual in human life has become deeper in our century. The resources available to schools in this quest have become richer and wider. However, an opposite tendency may be discerned in collective worship. While the quest for spirituality has become broader, the official understanding of the character of collective worship has become more constricted. Today this gap is so wide that it must be questioned whether, under the constraints which at present surround it, collective worship in school is able to make the contribution towards spirituality which is its prime purpose.

The subjective and objective meanings of worship

Like religion itself, worship has a subjective side. This is worship as indicating the desire of the heart: that which is taken seriously without qualification. 'As a hart pants after the water brooks, so thirsts my soul ....' The objective side of worship is that towards which worship is directed: '... after thee, O God'. These two aspects must always be held together.

In recent years the concept of 'collective worship' has served this function. 'Collective' has suggested the subjective side of worship, the range of attitudes and beliefs which are represented in a school gathering, whilst 'worship' has tended to indicate that towards which the activity is directed. Granted the disparity of beliefs and attitudes in Britain, and granted the non-confessional or educational context of the activity, it is inevitable that if closer definition of the objective aspect of worship is sought, the difficulty of holding the concept together will become greater. As the objective definition is tightened, the number of persons within the collectivity for whom it is an apt description necessarily shrinks.

An interminable process of definition

In 1988 an attempt was made to define the content of collective worship. This was followed by further demands for clarification and after five or six years of this process, it was impossible to deny that the ring had grown tighter and tighter. Theology itself has become captive to this process. When theology is used not so much to affirm life and liberty but to serve the purposes of legal constraint and the demand for inspection, it takes on a casuistic character. Each definition leads to another one.

This can be illustrated first with respect to God. The draft version of Circular 1/94 on 'Religious Education and Collective Worship' published by the Department for Education said that worship 'should be concerned with reverence or veneration paid to a being or power regarded as supernatural or divine' (para. 59). The final form of the Circular published on 31st January 1994 omits the word 'supernatural' and tells us that worship must be paid to a 'divine being or power' (para. 57). Is the divine being or power to be supernatural or not? If the divine being is not to be regarded as supernatural, then what we have seems to be rather pantheistic.

This attempt to offer a theological meaning for worship quickly led to a demand for further clarification. The Parental Alliance for Choice in Education asked the then Secretary of State to determine which divine being or power was being paid reverence or veneration (letter dated 10th June 1992 in connection with the Crowcroft Park Primary School controversy). This question, although inappropriate in the context of collective worship when correctly understood in its educational context, is surely perfectly legitimate, indeed irresistible, when the path of objective definition is being followed. In view of the fact that the acts of collective worship are to be 'wholly or mainly of a broadly Christian character' and that this is to be defined by seeing whether the collective worship 'reflects the broad traditions of Christian belief' (Education Reform Act 1988 7 (1,2)) it would not be surprising if the Secretary of State had given a clear reply. Within the broad traditions of Christian belief the name of the God to be worshipped is undoubtedly Father, Son and Holy Spirit. Perhaps wisely, the Secretary of State did not venture to go so far. He said that he did not have to discern the object of worship; it was sufficient to be reasonably satisfied that there was one (letter dated 7th July 1992).

This process went a step further with the publication in September 1994 of the OFSTED guidelines on the inspection of acts of collective worship to see whether they complied with the law. The guidelines indicate that the inspectors must establish that there has been 'a recognition of a divine being'. This is clearly unsatisfactory. First, it goes too far. Paragraph 57 of Circular 1/94 says that although worship is to be regarded as reverence or veneration paid to a supreme being or power, 'worship in schools will *necessarily* be of a different character'. If it will necessarily be of a different character, in what sense does the original definition or meaning apply? How can the OFSTED inspectors be advised to ascertain whether or not a supreme being or power has been recognized when the Department Circular they are following specifically says that what they are looking for will *necessarily* be of a different character?

On the other hand, the definition does not go far enough. The mere recognition of a divine being or power, even when reverence or veneration is offered to this divine being, is only *consistent* with the broad traditions of Christian belief and is not *distinctive* of them. If we may take it that the distinction between that which is consonant with the Christian tradition and that which is distinctive of it, applied as we shall see in a moment to the status of Jesus Christ, is also to apply to belief in God, then the guideline to the OFSTED inspectors is clearly inadequate. They must seek to establish that on a majority of days the deity who is recognized is none other than the Triune God of Christian faith.

It is clear that with paragraph 57 in the DfE Circular, the implicit contradiction within the concept of collective worship has become explicit. An inappropriate policy has been masked with an incoherent concept.

Not only are distinctions such as these inevitable with respect to the name and nature of the God to be worshipped, once the process of theological discrimination has begun, but they must also be applied to the sense in which the act of collective worship must 'contain some elements which relate specifically to the traditions of Christian belief and which accord a special status to Jesus Christ'. It was immediately clear that this was inadequate. What kind of status should be accorded to Jesus Christ? Should the word 'Christ' be taken seriously, and his Messianic status be affirmed? That would clearly exclude Jewish young people. Would it be sufficient to emphasize the status of Jesus as a teacher and prophet? That would enable both Jews and Muslims to be included.

On 16th June 1994 the Board of Deputies of British Jews wrote to the Secretary of State for Education seeking clarification. The reply is dated 14th July and says that 'the term broadly Christian as defined in section 7(2) of the 1988 Act does not, however, denote elements of worship which are merely consonant with Christianity, but which are distinctive of Christianity....' The letter continues: 'The element of Christianity which distinguishes it from other faiths is the status accorded to Jesus Christ, which is why this is mentioned in that part of the Circular.'

This interpretation makes it clear that the status of Jesus as teacher and prophet would not meet the requirements of the law. Jesus must be accorded the status which he has distinctively within the Christian faith, and that can only be his status as the incarnate Logos, the second person of the Trinity, true God of true God, begotten not made. The logic of this is as inevitable, given the process of theological definition, as the logic which must lead the Department to insist upon recognition of the True God.

A sad embarrassment

It is extraordinary that public servants should find themselves having to word letters of this kind. One cannot but sympathize with them in their evident embarrassment. The spiritual vision of school assembly has been lost beneath this mass of inquisitorial minutiae. Baroness Hooper, speaking for the Government in 1988, said that collective worship 'can perform an important function in binding together members of a school', while the then Bishop of London said that school worship must not 'break the school up into communities based on the various faiths of the parents'. This vision, of unity and community, of mutuality and participation, has been lost. It is no answer to point out that the determination procedure permits children from other religious backgrounds to avoid Christian worship. More determinations means more separations, more controversy, and more administrative complexity for the already overburdened schools. It is not surprising that the Churches Joint Education Policy Committee Working Party Report, published late in November 1994, describes a widespread sense of unease and suggests that 'collective assembly' might be preferable to collective worship. The Evangelical Alliance in its December 1994 statement said that collective worship is becoming unworkable. The teachers' unions are equally concerned.

A simple solution

It has become clear that section 7 of the 1988 Education Reform Act is deeply flawed. It is true that the Circular and the inspection process have made it much worse, but the root of the matter lies in the law itself. Section 7, the one which started the whole process of theological definition by requiring that collective worship should be of a Christian character, must go. Schools should be required to hold acts of collective spirituality. This expression would remove the controversies, the embarrassments and the divisions at a stroke. The link between spirituality and school assembly would be restored, and there would be an appropriate focus for the quest for spirituality which is being pursued so vigorously at the present time in the rest of the curriculum.

Chapter 4

The Agreed Syllabuses

The Agreed Syllabus: A Major Achievement

September 1971

*P*rior *to 1988, there was virtually no control over the content of the agreed syllabuses of religious education. Only the procedures were prescribed by law.*

The following extract is one of my earliest editorials, and was written at a time when religious education was increasingly considered to be the responsibility of the teacher. New educational research had increased the sense of professional responsibility, and changes in society meant that the days when the syllabus could be controlled by a group of theologians and clerics seemed long past. However, the significance of the local Conference, a place of dialogue between various sections of the community, was not as obvious as it became later. Similarly, it was more difficult in the early 1970s to appreciate the significance of local control, as opposed to the National Curriculum which emerged in 1988.

The agreed syllabus is one of the major achievements of religious education in England and Wales. The notion of agreement has been central since the inception of religious education in state schools, when the denominations agreed to exclude aspects of Christian faith which were distinctive of a particular denomination.

The syllabuses used in state schools in the later nineteenth century and in the early years of this century, often little more than lists of biblical passages, showed the constraints imposed upon the content of religious education by this negative form of agreement. But in the late twenties and early thirties panels of clergy, teachers and administrators showed what real co-operation could produce, and the agreed syllabuses of those years became, in many cases, authoritative manuals which inaugurated a new era in religious education.

What of the future?

Two major questions arise about the future pattern of agreed syllabuses. The first concerns the relationship between the churches and the religious education teaching profession. Although glad to co-operate and to receive advice, religious education specialists will be less and less willing to consent to a situation which allows the churches to prescribe and to veto what is taught in the classroom. It is contrary to the interests of religious education that its opponents should be able to say, as they now can, that the content of the subject is not entirely in the hands of educators. On the other hand, large sections of the public, including the humanist organizations as well as religious bodies, have an interest in religious education and it is right that this should be expressed in some effective manner, short of statutory control.

The second major question concerns the relationship between the agreed syllabuses and the processes of curriculum development as they are now understood. The emphasis upon teacher initiative and upon methods such as integration are not compatible with the practice of presenting to the teacher a syllabus in the creation of which he or she has had no direct part.

Religious syllabuses in the future should be compiled by teams of practising teachers working under the guidance of their own specialist colleagues. Representatives of churches and other interested bodies would attend the work sessions in an advisory capacity. The statutory form of the present syllabuses and the mechanism for assembling a Conference to draw up an agreed syllabus should be abandoned.

Widening the Religious Education Syllabus

January 1972

Although the teaching of World Religions was not required by law in the early 1970s (this did not happen until 1988) there was an enormous interest in this development. The Shap Working Party had been founded in 1969, stimulating much new work both in content and method.

The traditional approach towards the place in the religious education syllabus of religions other than Christianity is that other faiths are taught in the sixth form of the secondary school. Even a recent and enlightened agreed syllabus, that of the London Authority, *Learning for Life*, published in 1968, does not recommend serious study of non-Christian religions before the sixth form, although teachers are encouraged to include in the junior school the biographies of 'Benefactors of mankind: not only Christian but men of all beliefs who have helped their fellow men'. But there must have been many schools in London in 1968 where conditions were appropriate for the study of world religions long before pupils reached the sixth form.

Since the 1968 London syllabus there has been a considerable change in the climate of opinion, and we may now expect that religious syllabuses which do not pay serious attention to the major alternatives to Christianity will become increasingly rare, and that this will be true not only for middle and lower forms of the secondary school but even in the junior school.

A good deal of the credit for this broadening of the syllabus must go to the Shap Working Party on World Religions in Education. The work of members of the group is showing with increasing clarity that the fears and difficulties about this sort of teaching have often been exaggerated. It is both desirable and possible to introduce quite young pupils to certain aspects of various religions.

Of course, many problems are still being investigated. Some of these centre on issues which arise when members of other faiths are taught about their own religion in the county school. Some sections of the Christian community have found the move in recent years away from religious education as nurturing young people into faith towards a more descriptive and critical approach a difficult tendency to assimilate. There is little or no reason to think that leaders of the various non-Christian religious communities will find it any easier to understand exactly what are the potentials and the limits of the kind of religious education which the state schools ought to provide. Indeed, a critical approach, based on discussion and discovery methods, is often more alien to non-Christian traditional religious educational methods than it is to certain types of Christian catechesis.

We must proceed in the expectation that Islam will be taught to non-Muslim young people. Is the ordinary fifteen-year-old interested in the existence of God? If not, what makes us believe that he or she will be interested in Allah? Is it the novelty? Will the pupil's realization that the teacher is not trying to press his or her own personal beliefs create a greater readiness to learn?

Perhaps the most immediate danger is that in the teaching of Islam we might adopt methods abandoned in the teaching of Christianity. We might so easily teach Arabian geography and Persian history instead of their Syrian equivalents. We might so easily restore the linear syllabus based on chronological study, a method now largely discredited in study of the Bible. Perhaps the work done in presenting Christianity through pupil experiences and through discussion methods can be adapted to the teaching of Islam. Perhaps, on the other hand, the experience of teaching Islam will help us to think again about the techniques of creating the best learning conditions in the religious areas.

One thing we can be sure about: interest in teaching the world religions will increase. In this sphere, as in so many others, religious education continues to offer enormous stimulus and opportunity to the learning teacher.

The Importance of Teaching World Religions

September 1973

*B*y 1973, the Birmingham Agreed Syllabus Conference was well under way. This was to produce the first new agreed syllabus which fully foreshadowed the requirement of the 1988 Education Reform Act, in that although a range of world religions was recommended for study, every pupil was required to undertake study of Christianity, thus reflecting the fact that the principal religious traditions in Great Britain are in the main Christian, as the 1988 legislation was to express it.

It is mainly because of the emphasis on the teaching of many faiths that religious education is emerging as one of the growing points of friendly relations between immigrant peoples and the host community. Religious education has an important role to play in community relations in Britain today. But this can only be fulfilled if the religions concerned are treated with accuracy, with sympathy and with insight.

New interests for the teacher

For many teachers, the challenge of learning about another faith has refreshed and deepened their appreciation of their subject. The expansion of courses dealing with various faiths indicates the need and the popularity of such studies.

Integration

Many teachers are already finding that the possibilities for fruitfully including religion within integrated studies are vastly expanded when a number of faiths are offered by the religious education department.

Education sense

Perhaps the most important contribution made by the study of world religions is that a religious education is offered which makes some sense educationally. This breadth of content enables religious education to present itself to the curriculum as a study which comprises many of the hopes and fears of the majority of people today, and thus a subject worthy of the most humane and scholarly attention. If, as is increasingly the case, the non-religious lifestyles such as secular humanism and communism are added to the list, the importance of this cluster of subjects for the older adolescent can hardly be denied. Furthermore, enough text books and other aids are now available, enough practical suggestions have been made and enough experience has been won to show that teaching world religions and non-religious lifestyles is not a task for the sixth form only, nor even for the secondary school only. Like Christianity, the other faiths can also be taught in a limited way in the primary school.

Christians, humanists and world religions

Agreement between Christians and humanists has been made easier by the inclusion in the curriculum of religions other than Christianity and lifestyles other than religious ones. It is with some relief to both parties that the sharp and sometimes bitter debates of the sixties are seen to have died down. The world religions movement eases this tension. It does not resolve it completely and the relative calm of the Christian–humanist debate may be no more than a truce. There will continue to be different approaches from those who, although no longer wishing to generate faith in one religion or in religion as a whole, are generally sympathetic towards religion and convinced of its importance in the development of the human spirit, and those on the other hand who, although willing to accept a critical, descriptive study of religion, do not believe that it has much to offer the future. At least the discussion can now be about the actual desirability and the manner of religious education rather than about whether it is in any sense at all a proper educational activity.

Unsolved problems

Many young people find the study of various religions interesting. Most pupils in schools where Christianity is still the only religion taught before the sixth form would probably say, if asked, that they would like to study other faiths, but there is little evidence that when other religions have been studied pupils on the whole find them more interesting than Christianity and sometimes they appear less relevant.

This is not to suggest that we ought not to go on teaching the non-Christian faiths any more than it is to suggest that we ought not to go on teaching Christianity. Religious education must obviously press on, whatever the problems, with the presentation of its major content, the religions of the world.

But it does indicate that the problems facing religious education are connected with method as well as content. How can religion of any sort be made interesting and relevant to young people, many of whom are mundane in their interests and secular in their outlook? This will remain our chief classroom problem.

World religions and new methods

Much of the material on teaching other religions has been helpful in suggesting new methods, but it remains true that the interest in teaching world religions has so far been more creative in widening the content of the subject than in pioneering new methods of actually teaching it. It is easier to suggest what to teach than to show how to teach it, but as time goes by and more teachers turn to the new materials we can expect that more new ideas will be shared and more new methods will appear. It may be, for example, that the work units produced by the Schools Council Lancaster Project will stimulate many teachers to try to find new ways of teaching religion. It will be interesting to see whether, when the assumptions of the study of religion are brought to bear upon the teaching of Christianity itself, new insights into how to teach Christianity will appear.

Picking up the threads of the past?

In the meantime, there is a possibility that what was gained during the sixties will be forgotten. That would be a pity, because although it is true that some of what was done then was conceived in rather more specifically Christian terms than would now be possible in the county schools, such ideas as 'the problem-centred syllabus' and 'the life theme' represented great advances in the techniques of teaching religion. It is even possible that when the world religions content has been fully accepted and we can at last take for granted that Christianity is also a world religion, we will have to return to the work of Ronald Goldman and J.W.D. Smith, to pick up the threads where they left off. Their insights must not be lost but must be gathered up and adapted for religious education tomorrow.

Religions and Secular Life-stances

September 1974

With the widening of the religious education curriculum from Christianity to the principal religions, the question inevitably arose about the place of beliefs and commitments which were not obviously or mainly of a religious character. Many of the agreed syllabuses of today continue to include communism and humanism, and the following extract still stands as a explanation and a defence of this practice.

Communism and religious education

Defining the limits of the subject seems to be a current preoccupation of religious education. Until the late 1960s the main content was Christianity associated with moral education, social service and personal problems usually seen through Christian eyes. Since then the emphasis has been upon the human religious quest today, studied through a variety of religious traditions. The publicity given in the national press to the controversies surrounding the new Birmingham Agreed Syllabus has now given prominence to the possible inclusion of other ideologies and ways of life.

Religions and non-religions

Religious education should not be confined to the classical and traditional religions. It should deal with the faiths by which people live and 'faiths' should be interpreted in a broad way. Previous agreed syllabuses have made tentative steps in this direction. The Lancashire Agreed Syllabus of 1968 mentions 'Humanism' and 'Dialectical materialism' as possible discussion topics in the sixth form. In a somewhat similar context, the 1968 ILEA Syllabus refers to 'rationalism, materialism, Marxism, existentialism'. But in the syllabuses the non-religious ideologies were approached from the Christian point of view; they were thought of as 'challenges to faith' and were considered apologetically. The West Riding Syllabus of 1966 describes communism and humanism as 'Alternatives to the Christian faith' and the short book list consists of books about these alternatives written by Christians.

Recent trends

The tendency to include the non-religions in religious education received significant support in *The Fourth R* (The Durham Report) in 1970. 'By religion we mean some pattern of belief and behaviour related to the questions of ultimate concern. For some, it is an Eastern religion; for some it is Christianity; for others it is agnostic humanism; for many it may be little more than moral stoicism. Man seems to have to find "a faith to live by" ' (p. 100). *Religious Education in Secondary Schools* (Schools Council Working Paper 36, 1971) remarks: 'It may be argued that some of the alternatives to religious faith, such as secular humanism, Marxism, and Maoism deserve the same sympathetic study and attention. We would agree' (p. 66). There is a well-established group of new textbooks for religious education which deals with the non-religions alongside the religions (e.g. F.G. Herod, *What Men Believe,* and Sherratt and Hawkin, *Gods and Men).* The new Birmingham Syllabus goes much further than its predecessors in that the Handbook provides fairly detailed courses for the fifth form in both communism and humanism, and accepts the advice given by Working Paper 36 that such beliefs should receive 'the same sympathetic study' as the religions themselves.

Supplementing the religions

Study of the non-religions should not take the place of studying the religions but should expand, enrich and supplement it. The Birmingham Syllabus, for example, offers major and minor courses in the non-religions. The question is not whether we should yield up the central place in religious education to humanism and communism but whether the non-religions provide an appropriate and even a necessary context for religious studies.

Religion or politics?

We are not here concerned with political education directly but with the religions and the non-religions, quasi-religious or non-religious stances for living. The politicization of religious education is to do with the sensitivity of the religions and those who teach them towards all human life on earth. It is not a matter of exchanging the study of religions for the study of politics.

How then can distinctions be made between the religions and non-religions which are a suitable context for religious education classes, and the political movements which are suitable for classes in political education? It would be naive (or shrewd) to suggest that such distinctions can be made easily or clearly. Some religions have a political expression and some political movements have a religious expression. Christianity may take a political form, as the Christian Democratic parties on the continent of Europe illustrate. Much of the Christian theology coming from the Americas is radically political in the inferences it draws from faith. Relationships between Islam and the state and between Judaism and Zionism indicate a similar political consciousness on the part of those two religions. Communism, on the other hand, although dominated by more immediate political concerns has some of the characteristics of a religion.

The fact that the Birmingham Syllabus selects communism and humanism shows clearly that the intention is not to teach politics. Humanism has less of a political expression than either Christianity or communism. These two movements have been chosen because they have similarities to the religions; they are both whole stances for living. The fact that one of them happens also to be a potent political force is, from the point of view of the religious educator, interesting but incidental.

Three criteria for selecting non-religions

Three questions must be asked about any candidate for inclusion within a religious education syllabus. First, does the ideology or way of life explicitly reject religion? Second, does it claim to be a substitute for religion? Third, does it, nevertheless, exhibit certain features typical of religion, such as a theory of history, a total view of the human and its destiny and a system of ethics? These criteria are not inconsistent. It is precisely because they have similarities to the religions that the non-religious stances for living can offer themselves as substitutes to religion.

Fascism?

Communism, humanism and fascism may qualify for inclusion. So perhaps may some of the movements within the counter-culture, such as the LSD lifestyle advocated by Timothy Leary. Existentialism of the type associated with Albert Camus and Jean-Paul Sartre may also be included. But these criteria, although a necessary ground for inclusion, do not constitute a sufficient ground.

Fascism, for example, although it may satisfy the criteria, may be thought insufficiently significant in Britain to warrant a place in a hard-pressed curriculum, or it may be deemed morally unworthy of inclusion.

Labour, Liberal and Conservative?

The mainstream British political parties are clearly excluded by our three criteria. These political parties, in spite of the various beliefs which they represent, remain essentially pragmatic. The change in any opposition when it becomes a government confirms this. They do have their philosophies but they are purely political philosophies. The Liberals do not offer themselves as a substitute for the religions, the Conservatives do not claim a comprehensive interpretation of every aspect of life, the Labour party does not explicitly reject any doctrine of Christianity. If there are religious influences upon these parties (such as the relation between Methodism and the trade union movement) this would be approached as part of Christian Studies.

Capitalism?

There are bound to be many ambiguous cases and capitalism is one of them. Perhaps it would be useful to make the same sort of distinction between the explicit and the implicit in the study of the non-religious stance for living. No doubt it is full of all sorts of religious and non-religious implications for living. But it is controlled by desire for profits. It does not meet any of the three criteria *prima facie* and therefore it should probably be excluded. Capitalism implies a view of the human but it does not preach a doctrine of the human. It adopts an attitude towards the world but it has no teaching about the world. In these respects it differs from communism.

Why the non-religions should be included

It is increasingly being argued that the modern study of theology must be contextual. The meaning of faith today can only be determined when religious faith is placed in dialogue with the whole of human life in the world today. This view of the way theology should be carried on has implications for the teaching of religion and non-religion in schools and is becoming another notable example of the influence of theology in universities upon religious education.

We may also argue that the perspective which pupils may have of Christianity is limited if they know nothing of the non-Christian religions and similarly the perspective which they have of religion as a whole is limited if they know nothing of the great secular movements of today. It is part of all pupils' understanding of religion that they should understand why religion is rejected. Part of their appreciation of life with God is their appreciation of life without God. To offer religious education as assisting the pupil in developing a meaning of life but to make no reference to the secular meanings would be to offer the pupil an unnecessarily restricted view of the meanings which people find in their lives today.

Finally, the non-religious stances for living are worthy in many cases of being studied for their own sake and quite apart from any light which they may throw upon religion. They represent a significant segment of the things for which people live.

The context for religious education

An implication of the innate value of the non-religious lifestyles is that religious education may not be the only part of the curriculum which should examine them. They do not always have to be seen in relation to the religions. Communism and humanism, for example, may very well be taught within history, social studies, economics or literature classes. A subject like humanism is suitable for inclusion within religious education but that does not mean that religion need make an exclusive claim for it.

It must also be realized that the context within which religion is studied is provided not only by the religious education syllabus but by the curriculum as a whole. There is then a good case for claiming that there should continue to be religious education departments staffed by teachers who are specialists in religion, but that the context of these studies, whether within the department or within the whole curriculum should be the whole range of belief and commitment.

Christian fears

Doubts about the inclusion of the non-religious stances for life come from two quarters, and they centre mainly upon communism. There is a considerable body of Christian opinion which is doubtful, and this viewpoint must be respected. There is also a considerable political opposition which must not be respected at all.

The debate between Christians turns upon questions involving the Christian response to secularism and the nature of the Christian mission today. The character of the Christian witness in education is also a crucial problem. These are matters about which Christians of equally deep faith and vision may at present differ. We must seek guidance from each other and from the Holy Spirit.

Political opposition

The political opposition turns upon the difficulty which some politicians seem to have of understanding what teaching is all about. The politicians in mind assume that if a teacher teaches Christianity, it is because the teacher is a Christian and wants to encourage others to be so. The politician assumes that if a teacher teaches communism the same motivation applies. It does not seem to occur to these politicians that the teacher is not an evangelist or a propagandist but simply an educator. Just as the preachers used to interpret the classroom in terms of their pulpits, so now these politicians interpret the classroom in terms of the hustings. If the arguments about the Birmingham Syllabus have demonstrated anything, it is that as far as some politicians are concerned, teaching is still hardly a profession.

Agreed Syllabuses since the 1988 Education Reform Act (I)

Autumn 1989

In the summer of 1988, when I began to read the religious education sections of the 1988 Education Reform Act for myself, I was surprised to discover that it bore little resemblance to what the press and media had led me to expect. The wording was far more ambiguous than I had anticipated, and it was soon clear that I and the country as a whole had been led astray by a propaganda spin given to the words by the Christian right wing. Robert Jackson studied this in his important article 'The Misrepresentation of Religious Education' *in M. Leicester and M.J. Taylor (eds),* Ethics, Ethnicity and Education *(London, Kogan Page, 1992, pp. 100–113).*

The publicity had given the impression that the world religions or multi-religious syllabuses of the preceding fifteen years were now illegal and that future syllabuses would concentrate almost entirely upon teaching Christianity. My reading of the Act, however, made me realize that the reverse was the true situation: the previous syllabuses had been confirmed, and the relationship between the teaching of Christianity and the teaching of the other religions was to be pretty much what it had been before. It was necessary, in the circumstances, to offer a fairly detailed exegesis of the text of the legislation, and this was first published in the extract which follows. Much of this material appeared in my explanatory booklet The Act Unpacked.

Although the requirement that new agreed syllabuses should 'reflect the fact that the religious traditions in Great Britain are in the main Christian whilst taking account of the teaching and practices of the other principal religions represented in Great Britain' (section 8(3)) is certainly a new form of words, it only confirms professional practice as it has developed over the past twenty years, namely, that agreed syllabuses should be multi-faith in approach but with an appropriate emphasis upon the Christian religious traditions. The syllabuses prior to 1965 will be most in need of revision, since these older syllabuses tend to be Christian based. Not only do these older syllabuses generally fail to take account of other religions, but their treatment of Christianity itself tends to be biblical, historical and monolithic, whereas the 1988 requirement suggested an emphasis upon Christian plurality and contemporaneity.

Further evidence in support of this interpretation, if any were needed, became available. The Religious Education Council of England and Wales published its *Handbook for Agreed Syllabus Conferences, SACREs and Schools* in which twenty-three syllabuses from the period 1973–87 were analysed. Appendix 1 presented the result of the analysis of the aims and objectives of these syllabuses, and showed that fifteen of the syllabuses specifically included the aim 'to appreciate Christianity and the Christian tradition' while thirteen (not necessarily different from the first group) have as an aim 'to explore world religions and to understand living in a multi-faith society'. It must not be concluded that there were eight syllabuses which do not prescribe Christianity: this religion is always included in the syllabuses whether or not it is actually mentioned in the aims.

Appendix 2 analysed the curriculum content of these syllabuses, showing that for the infant and early junior years nineteen syllabuses included 'events/teaching of Jesus and/or early Christianity' while only four syllabuses included 'stories from Buddhism, Hinduism, Islam and Sikhism'. Of the fourteen syllabuses surveyed for the top junior and lower secondary years, only three included a study of one or more world religions other than Christianity. For the post-fourteen secondary years twenty-three syllabuses were surveyed, of which six included one or more world religions other than Christianity while seventeen specifically emphasized Christianity. In the remaining five syllabuses Christianity was included in a range of topic work.

If one had been trying to summarize the objectives and content of the recent syllabuses, it could hardly have been done more accurately than by saying that they 'reflect the fact that the religious traditions in Great Britain are in the main Christian whilst taking account of the teaching and practices of the other principal religions'.

The first new agreed syllabus

The first agreed syllabus to appear since the new Act came into force has now been published. It comes from the London Borough of Ealing. It is a world religions syllabus, with an emphasis upon the study of Christianity but including substantial education in the Sikh faith (the area includes Southall which is a major centre of the Sikh community in Britain) as well as Hinduism, Islam and other principal religions. BBC Radio 4 on July 2 announced the rather surprising news that this syllabus is being criticized by some people as being contrary to the new Act and there has even been a suggestion that the matter might be taken to court as a test case. The same radio programme ('Sunday') included the comments from a teacher in a junior school in the borough who explained that 93 per cent of her children were from religions other than Christianity, especially Sikhs. There were, she remarked, only four children in the school from Christian families, and she thus considered the syllabus very appropriate since it included both the teaching of Christianity which is suitable for all British children as well as the study of Sikhism which is an important affirmation and exploration of the family background of many of the pupils.

The previous Ealing Syllabus, from 1948, was an exclusively Christian syllabus badly in need of revision along the lines suggested by the new Act. It is understood that work on the new Ealing syllabus was well under way before the introduction of the 1988 legislation, but it is a model of the kind of revision which would in the next few years take place in many of the local education authorities. In the West Midlands, for instance, one authority was still relying upon the 1966 West Riding Agreed Syllabus, which fails to deal adequately with the teaching and practices of the other principal religions and is far from meeting the needs of the community it now serves.

A strange misunderstanding?

It is being pointed out that, although confirmation and encouragement of the approach of the more recent agreed syllabuses is the obvious result of the new legislation and is the plain teaching of its words, this was not, so it is said, the intention of those who urged that Christianity should be named in the Bill when the legislation was passing through the House of Lords in the spring and summer of 1988. A careful reading of Hansard makes it clear that some of these people in the House of Lords did indeed think that they were changing religious education curriculum practice rather than confirming it. They seem to have seen themselves as reformers, and the Act is called the 'Education *Reform* Act'. Allegations that Christianity was being neglected were flying thick and fast and the excellent work being done in community relations through religious education was denounced as a 'mish-mash'. Two or three anecdotes of doubtful veracity but spectacular in their emotional impact were used to inflame the passions, but while a number of powerful groups such as the Church of England were consulted in order to reach agreement about the actual wording of the legislation little was done to seek advice from inspectors and advisers in the field. Did not the reformers who wanted religious education to reflect the fact that the religious traditions in Great Britain are in the main Christian know that religious education syllabuses were already reflecting this fact? Did they not know of the resurgence of interest in the teaching of Christianity which has been going on for about ten years? Had they not studied the lists of the principal publishers of religious education textbooks for schools to note the many new books and entire series dealing with Christianity, and to observe the preponderance of books on Christianity over books dealing with other major religions? Is it possible that they were badly informed?

Moreover, if their intention was, as they say, to reject the world religions 'mish-mash' and to concentrate the religious education curriculum upon the centrality of Christianity as foundation and basis, how could it be that the legislation which they passed did not articulate this intention but rather confirmed current practice and is now encouraging the production of multi-faith syllabuses? Can it be that a government might be so incompetent as to produce legislation opposed to its own intentions? If those intentions were ill-advised and uninformed, the fact that the legislation confounded the intentions of the legislators must be attributed to the overriding mercy of a benevolent deity.

How to 'reflect the fact'

Let us look a little more closely at the implications for the curriculum of the now famous words. It is important to emphasize that nothing is said which would suggest that the agreed syllabuses should be *confined* to reflecting the 'fact that ... whilst taking account of...'. The law says that they shall do this, *not* that they shall do nothing else. It is thus perfectly in order for agreed syllabuses to recommend the study of religions which are not principal religions, and there may be many situations in which this would have an educational advantage. There is much to be learnt, for example, from the religions of primal societies, from the religious symbols and mythologies of ancient Greece, Rome and Egypt, as well as from other religions (like that of the Parsees) which have important spiritual and ethical lessons for humanity. Moreover, there is nothing in the wording which requires that any new agreed syllabuses should be organized around the systematic treatment of religion. It is generally agreed in religious education curriculum development that the so-called 'systems approach' can have a significant place in religious learning but it is not the only one, and the very fact that it is so systematic can have serious disadvantages, especially for younger children. It would be perfectly possible to devise an approach through a variety of themes and topics involving religious and cross-cultural local and national issues which would adequately reflect Christianity and take account of other religions.

What is required is not that Christianity should be taught, outlined or presented in a simple and direct manner but that a certain fact should be reflected. What is to be reflected is not even Christianity itself but the fact that the religious traditions of a certain physical-political area have a certain character. They are, in the main, Christian. It is no accident that Christianity as such is not mentioned. This is because the teaching of Christianity is to be mediated through such realities as tradition, significance and area. It is through these realities that the curriculum is to *reflect* Christianity. The mediation suggests the indirect character of this influence which is also inferred by the word 'reflect' itself. Naturally, this does not mean that pupils will not have direct teaching about Christianity. We are not talking about classroom activity, or schemes of work, but about a principle which is to be reflected when an entire syllabus is being constructed.

In an address given to members of West Midlands SACREs on 1st July 1989, Dr Michael Grimmitt, referring to the NFER/REC Report *Religious Education, Values and Worship, 1988*, indicated that 'reflect' could mean possessing an overall quantity superiority, i.e. a syllabus might recommend 51 per cent of its content to be devoted to the Christian traditions, leaving 49 per cent to be distributed amongst the remaining religions. It could also mean that of all religions included, Christianity should be the most significant, i.e. if Christianity occupied 20 per cent of the curriculum, each of five other religions could occupy exactly 16 per cent. Moreover, we might ask whether this or some other kind of reflection must prevail equally at every phase of the curriculum. It would, for example, be perfectly possible for a syllabus to deal exclusively with Christianity (or some other faith) for an entire year and not to mention it at all during the following year, provided that the overall effect could be described as a reflection. With the other religions, it is specified that their teaching and their practices are to be studied, while with Christianity nothing is said about any sub-division of Christian content, thus leaving a certain vagueness about the manner of teaching Christianity.

Grimmitt also pointed out that this kind of content calculation is not the only way that reflection might occur. It would be quite possible to present a variety of religious aspects and issues drawing illustrations from a range of religious traditions, making sure that a sufficient number of the illustrations were from Christian sources. Grimmitt pointed out that although it was sometimes claimed that the required reflection suggests that Christianity might provide a theological or philosophical basis for the entire process of curriculum development, this would be going far beyond the natural meaning of the words. In view of the fact that the construction of the agreed syllabus is in the hands of local Conferences and that the local SACREs are responsible for the recommendation of methods of teaching and teacher training, it is clear that the wording must be interpreted as only a very general guideline.

The importance of the local community

The balance between the legal guideline and the local community must be carefully borne in mind. The way in which 'reflection' and 'taking into account' are expressed will be a product both of the general situation in Great Britain and of the local characteristics. No local education authority can fail to take account of the other religions even if these are not significantly present in the local area. In the same way no authority dominated by religions other than Christianity can fail to reflect the Christian traditions. In an area, a school or a group of schools in which most or all of the pupils are from religious families other than Christian, there is no reason at all why appropriate reflection of the Christian traditions should require that Christianity should be taught more than any other religion. In such schools and areas, the local needs of the community might require an emphasis upon the local religions. If Christianity figured merely as one of these, but was not very important in the actual school, it might be enough to have a syllabus in which Christianity occupied no more space than any other religion, and was outweighed overall by the other religions put together. This could be the local schools' way of reflecting the fact that in the country as a whole the Christian traditions are more significant.

The 'other' religions

The same range of possibilities exists for the way in which agreed syllabuses might take account of the other principal religions. It is significant that the guideline does not refer to the principal religions *of* Great Britain but to the principal religions *represented* in Great Britain. Nothing is said about the criteria which would lead to a religion being 'principal' nor how many adherents such a religion would have to have before it could be regarded as being 'represented in Great Britain'. Nothing is said about how many of these principal religions there might be; we are not told that the syllabuses must take account of *all* of them, nor that they should be dealt with systematically one by one. This is all available for local deliberation.

Finally, it is worth remembering that there has always been a space between the agreed syllabus of the local education authority and the scheme of work actually taught in particular schools. The agreed syllabuses have never regarded themselves as all-embracing statements of curriculum for religious education, but as offering general guidelines. Indeed, there have been agreed syllabuses in the past where more content has been suggested than could possibly be included adequately by any one school, in order to insist upon the responsibility of the teachers themselves in the selection and arrangement of suitable material. The usual practice has been to advise that what a school teaches must be contained in or must be consistent with the agreed syllabus, but it has not been normal to insist that everything suggested by the agreed syllabus should be taught. This is how the requirement that religious education should be offered 'in accordance with' an agreed syllabus has traditionally been interpreted. Teaching can be in accordance with something or other in many and varied ways.

Agreed Syllabuses since the 1988 Education Reform Act (II)

Summer 1991

Within a couple of years it had become clear to the Christian right wing that their 1988 attempt to turn religious education into mainly Christian education was not succeeding. The ambiguity of the legislation had become all too clear. However, many attempts were made between 1990 and 1994 to restore their own monocultural interpretation of the legislation. All of these failed, but frequently the propaganda spin gave the impression that they had succeeded. It was not until the publication of the so-called Model Syllabuses by the School Curriculum and Assessment Authority (SCAA) on 5th July 1994 that it became highly clear that the pluralistic interpretation of the Act had come to stay. In the following extract the tenses remain unchanged, so as to give the present-day reader an insight into the issues as they appeared to me in early 1991, when it was first written.

Since the 1988 Education Reform Act came into force, seven new agreed syllabuses have been adopted. This is not a large number, but a few tentative conclusions may be drawn. Several of the syllabuses were in a fairly advanced state before the legislation came into effect, and it is noteworthy that in every case they could be quite easily adapted to the requirements. This suggests that the main impact of the Act will be to confirm existing emphases within the best professional practice, i.e. the legislation is better seen as providing for continuity than for reform. The Act requires that the syllabuses should provide for the study of several religions and all the new syllabuses reflect this.

There continues to be controversy as to whether the new syllabuses adequately reflect the fact that the principal religious traditions of Great Britain are in the main Christian. On 24th April 1990 the Education Curriculum Complaints Panel of the London Borough of Ealing dismissed a complaint against its recently adopted agreed syllabus. The panel took the view that the recommended balance between Christianity and other religions was not inconsistent with the requirements of the Act and that the general style and recommendations about teaching methods in the syllabus were appropriate for local conditions and would be supported by additional guidelines to be provided by the Local Education Authority. A similar complaint against the London Borough of Newham was also unsuccessful, and the complainants have now sought the advice of the Secretary of State.

In the 1970s and 1980s religious education not only in England and Wales but in Scotland and Northern Ireland as well had become a significant focus of the search for understanding and reconciliation between the various religious communities settled in Britain. A theology of dialogue was created by leading representatives of several faiths, working from their own religious positions but meeting in the common ground of religious education. In 1988 there was considerable concern lest the search for common ground and mutual understanding should be overtaken by religious interests of a more monocultural kind. There was much in the public debates which accompanied the new educational legislation which justified this nervousness. By 1989, however, it had become apparent that the religious clauses of the Act were expressed in such a way that the educational and multicultural interests of the subject would not only continue but might find encouragement. The experience of the last year or so has confirmed this hope. A broad, educational interpretation of the legislation is gaining ground all the time.

In this context, it was rather disturbing to read that on 12th December 1990 an Early Day Motion appeared on the Order Paper in the House of Commons, EDM No. 225, which was headed 'RE in Maintained Schools' and read as follows:

> That this House recalls that agreed syllabuses for religious education in maintained schools must now statutorily reflect the 'mainly Christian' religious traditions in Great Britain, whilst taking account of the other principal religions now represented here; believes that religious education in schools should respect the integrity and identity of each religion studied, and should promote respect, understanding, and tolerance for those adhering to different faiths; further believes that thematic teaching approaches which blur the distinctions between religions tend to undermine their coherence and should be avoided; recognises that for good educational reasons only two, or at the very most three, religions can be studied in any worthwhile depth within the constraints imposed on religious education by schools' weekly timetables; urges the Secretary of State for Education and Science to monitor, assess, and if necessary, correct local education authority syllabuses in this field to ensure the reflection in those syllabuses of these foregoing principles; and further urges the Secretary of State to issue supplementary guidance to local education authorities on the subject.

The motion was not debated in the House, because the government decided that it would be premature to have such a discussion whilst the Secretary of State was still thinking about the agreed syllabus matters which had been brought before him.

One of the main reasons why the government did not want religious education to become a subject of the National Curriculum was because it was thought undesirable that the Secretary of State should have to adjudicate on matters concerning the content and method of teaching in religious education. It was decided to delegate these matters to parents, teachers and city councillors at the local level. The local Standing Advisory Councils for Religious Education (SACREs) are responsible for giving advice on teaching methods, while responsibility for content lies with the authorities themselves upon the recommendation of their Agreed Syllabus Conferences. If the House of Commons were ever to have a debate on some such motion, and were the Secretary of State to be placed under this kind of pressure as a result, there would undoubtedly be renewed demand for religious education to be fully integrated into the National Curriculum and to be protected by the due processes of consultation from which the other subjects now benefit. Moreover, the Secretary of State would surely be unable to advise in this area without receiving his own advice from the National Curriculum Council or some other body representing the LEAs and the SACREs. The government would not wish to be led into these difficult and controversial areas, and we must hope that Members of Parliament will resist the temptation to become in their own debating chamber a sort of national SACRE.

Collective worship

It is more difficult to assess the situation with respect to collective worship. The National Curriculum Council is currently preparing and is expected shortly to publish its first views of SACRE annual reports. It is expected that these will offer some indication of the kinds of determination which SACREs have offered, and may contain other information about the conduct of collective worship. SACREs are required to submit to the Secretary of State annual returns giving details about their determinations. Once again, we may hope that some public statement will be made about these submissions in due course.

In the meantime, the general situation is somewhat similar to that of classroom religious education. An early fear that the emphasis upon Christianity would create unmanageable tensions and divisions within schools has diminished. The vast majority of schools have maintained a balanced, educational interpretation of collective worship and have seen the Act as permitting and perhaps even strengthening multicultural and inter-faith perspectives. The Secretary of State is currently considering complaints about collective worship in three schools. Two of these, primary schools in Bradford and Wakefield, have been before the Secretary of State for about a year and the third case came along late in 1990. In every case, the complaints had been considered and dismissed locally.

Acton School, a thriving comprehensive school in the London Borough of Ealing, had obtained a determination from its SACRE on the part of the entire school in order to enable it to have acts of collective worship which would continue to draw upon all the religious traditions represented in the school. On 22nd November 1990 the Educational Curriculum Complaints Panel of the LEA listened to the evidence. The complaint was that multi-faith worship is not consistent with the requirements of the 1988 Act whether this takes place under a SACRE determination or not. Dismissing the complaint, the Panel emphasized the responsibility of the school itself to decide what form its collective worship should take when once the requirement that the broad traditions of Christian belief should be reflected had been lifted by a determination of SACRE. There was no evidence that the school had not acted responsibly and with appropriate consultation in determining its policy. As far as the kind of worship envisaged or permitted by the Act itself is concerned, the Panel took the view that a broad and realistic interpretation in the interests of local community life was fully within the intention and the wording of the legislation. It will be interesting to see what view the Secretary of State takes on these matters, but it is difficult to see what grounds could be found for overthrowing these local recommendations.

The SACREs

It has become clear that the most important and beneficial change brought about by the 1988 Act has been the mandatory status of the Standing Advisory Councils on Religious Education. After an initial period of uncertainty and confusion, many SACREs are now functioning well, and as a group they are growing in confidence. While some LEAs continue to be suspicious of their SACRE and to starve it of resources, many are seeing in SACRE one of the most significant responsibilities which Local Education Authorities still have. In some of the larger SACREs, the appointment of SACRE clerks to work with local inspectors and religious education advisers is providing much-needed administrative support, and the fact that members of many SACREs are now meeting each other regularly is helping to form a nationwide body of opinion which will probably become increasingly influential. The next step must be for the government, which has so successfully begun to reinvigorate religious education at the local level, to resource the SACREs to carry out their assigned task.

Side effects of the legislation

Many of the most important consequences of the legislation have been indirect. The way that the subjects of the National Curriculum have been developing through attainment targets, programmes of study and forms of assessment has been a significant stimulus to religious education teachers. A flurry of working parties, reports and projects bears witness to this increase in activity, and this is all to the good. The pity is that it has all been carried out on a shoestring, using mainly voluntary resources, supported sometimes by very small funding from LEAs. The resourcing of innovation and development in religious education remains a major cause of concern.

Whatever might be argued about the effect of the Act on marginalizing religious education, it is undoubtedly the case that huge sums of public money have been put into rethinking and retraining in the National Curriculum subjects while religious education, in spite of all the promises made in 1988, has been largely left to struggle on alone. This is not the deal which the nation or the profession thought it was getting in 1988.

Should Agreed Syllabuses Be Mainly Christian?

Autumn 1991

Interpretation of the legal requirements for new agreed syllabuses remains a problem for the local Conferences whose duty it is to prepare these. The remaining three sections of this chapter deal with this problem. In the one which follows, I take up the question of the 1991 controversy which centred on the legality of the Ealing and Newham syllabuses, and the interpretation which the then Department of Education and Science issued in March. Once again, the tenses remain unchanged, so as to indicate the state which the discussion had reached. Some of the later parts of this editorial were published in my short article 'Agreed Syllabuses and the Law' *in* Resource *(Vol. 14, No. 1, pp. 1–3).*

All agreed syllabuses published after 29th September 1988 must 'reflect the fact that the religious traditions in Great Britain are in the main Christian whilst taking account of the teaching and practices of the other principal religions represented in Great Britain' as prescribed by the 1988 Education Reform Act section 8(3). On 18th March 1991 the Secretary of State delivered his long-awaited advice regarding the complaint which had been received that the newly published agreed syllabuses of the London Boroughs of Ealing and Newham did not adequately reflect this section. On the same date, the Department of Education and Science sent to all Chief Education Officers and others a letter in which the Secretary of State passed on the advice which he had received concerning the interpretation of section 8(3).

The press reaction

The first the public knew about this correspondence was in the national press on Friday, 22nd March. The headline in *The Times* was 'Clarke urges emphasis on Christian education', while the *Guardian* reported 'Schools told to focus on Bible'. On 29th March the *Ealing Borough Recorder* told us that 'Christian tradition is upheld' and on 12th April the *Ealing and Southall Informer* said that 'Kenneth Clarke backs Christianity in schools'. The *Daily Star* had summed up the general response as follows: '... now education authorities throughout Britain – whatever their feelings about Jesus – will *have* to teach our kids about Him. It is a famous victory for parents, for Christians – and for commonsense. Britain may now be a multicultural country *but that does not mean British culture should be banned from the classroom*' (emphasis original).

In its own more measured way, the report in *The Times,* the headline of which has already been quoted, was equally misleading. 'Schools should devote most attention to Christianity in religious education, Kenneth Clarke ... has insisted in a letter circulated to education officers.'

It was not until Monday, 25th March that the general letter from the Department of Education and Science was available in most Local Education Authority offices. When the contents were compared with the press treatment of the previous week, there was some feeling of surprise. Contrary to what the press had said, the letter contains no particular emphasis upon Christianity. It does not suggest that insufficient attention has been paid to Christianity; nor does it demand that more attention should be paid. Indeed, the advice is that an agreed syllabus 'cannot exclude from its teaching any of the principal religions represented in Great Britain' and 'cannot confine itself exclusively to religious education based on Christian traditions'. One should not test the legality of a new agreed syllabus by asking whether it is 'mainly Christian'. None of these expressions, which give balance to the legal advice, was reported in the press, and it is important to notice that both *The Times* and the *Guardian* published letters and articles correcting the misinterpretation.

'Please give full particulars'

The emphasis in the 18th March letter was not upon Christianity, nor upon other religions, which is why it is impossible to test the legality of agreed syllabuses against 'such shorthand phrases as "mainly Christian" or "multifaith" '. Rather, the ruling is that agreed syllabuses are not to be vague. A syllabus 'which is to meet the statutory requirements must give sufficient particulars' to show that 8(3) is being carried out. Thus, the 'traditions, practices and teaching of Christianity and other major religions must be set out, and the syllabus should 'indicate which of such matters should appropriately be taught at various ages and times'.

In other words, it is not sufficient merely to say in the agreed syllabus that teachers should make sure that their teaching reflects the fact that the principal religious traditions in Great Britain are in the main Christian and take account of the teaching and practices of the other principal religions represented in Great Britain. The mere repetition of these words is insufficient. It is not enough to have a syllabus which offers aims and objectives for the subject, sets out a variety of approaches, offers remarks about resources and so forth. The syllabuses are to be content-centred, as section 8(3) requires, and that content must be made articulate so as to 'give sufficient guidance to the reader, and thus the teacher, as to *what* [emphasis added] Christian traditions, learning, teaching and festivals are going to be taught and what elements are going to be taught in respect of the other principal religions represented in Great Britain'. The emphasis is to be not upon how, or why, but upon *what,* i.e. upon the particularity of content.

The balance between Christianity and other principal religions

Let us now return to the question with which we began: Are the agreed syllabuses to be mainly Christian? This brings us to the question of balance. At this point the legal advice introduces two new expressions: 'reasonable amount of attention' and 'properly reflected'. In all cases, agreed syllabuses 'must devote a reasonable amount of attention to teaching based on Christian traditions'. But what is 'a reasonable amount'?

The answer to this cannot be determined precisely. The reason for this is while 'the fact that the religious traditions in Great Britain are in the main Christian would *in most cases* [emphasis added] be properly reflected by devoting most attention to Christian traditions', there will be other cases where this will not be so. This is because an agreed syllabus 'cannot confine itself exclusively to religious education based on Christian traditions or exclude from its teaching any of the principal religions represented in Great Britain'. The determination of this balance will lie at the local level.

It is this element of local responsibility which leads to the concept not of pure reflection or simple reflection, but *proper* (emphasis added) reflection. Proper reflection may sometimes mean that teaching about Christianity will not occupy most of the syllabus. Most will be devoted to the teachings of the other principal religions. The balance being determined locally may go one way or the other. This is why the question to be put is not whether the syllabus is mainly Christian or is multi-faith but whether local decisions have been reasonably made.

The result will continue to be a balance. Balances may swing a little this way or that but must not tip too far. A syllabus which contained a great deal of attention paid to the teachings of the other principal religions but hardly any detail regarding Christianity would not be balanced, and the same would be true the other way. A syllabus which was mainly Christian and which devoted scant attention to the other principal religions, or failed to give sufficient details to guide the teacher in the presentation of any principal religion, would be unbalanced.

The Ealing decision

The same imbalance is found in the press reports dealing with the Secretary of State's advice to the London Borough of Ealing. The *Greenford and Northolt Gazette* for 29th March quotes the MP for Ealing North, Mr Harry Greenway, as saying that the syllabus 'was clearly defective in that it did not refer to Jesus, God or the Bible anywhere'. It could equally be claimed that the syllabus was defective because it did not refer to Krishna, Allah and the *Guru Granth Sahib* anywhere. Mr Greenway's argument is misleading. He and others had complained that the Ealing Syllabus was insufficiently Christian. He gets a reply advising that the syllabus is insufficiently detailed about anything; he then announces that his point of view has prevailed.

This can be confirmed quite easily by turning to the letter from the Department of Education and Science to the Ealing Authority of 18th March. In the first place, even the nature of the complaint received by the Department does not agree with the descriptions offered by Mr Greenway. '... the Secretary of State has been considering a complaint that the new agreed syllabus adopted by the Authority does not comply with section 8(3) of the Education Reform Act 1988'. The letter goes on to quote the section and to point out that any syllabus adopted now must comply with this section. Nothing is said about a complaint having been received to the effect that the syllabus was insufficiently Christian, or did not mention Jesus, God or the Bible. Paragraph 8 of the Department of Education and Science letter concludes that the Ealing syllabus 'gives insufficient guidance ... as to the day-to-day content of the religious education and how the content, balance and mix referred to in section 8(3) is to be achieved'. Nothing whatever is said about the syllabus failing to comply with the law because it was insufficiently Christian. The advice goes on to say that the syllabus fails to comply because it does not indicate what aspects of Christianity and what elements of the other principal religions are to be taught. It is insufficiently particular about anything.

Nothing is said in the letter about the spirit or the intentions of the Ealing syllabus, although we note the significant comment that it should not 'be designed to convert pupils, or to urge a particular religion or religious belief on pupils'. The fact that Ealing adopted a particular balance appropriate to its schools and a particular educational philosophy towards religious education is nowhere criticized in the letter. The vigorous defence of the Ealing Syllabus by Revd Neil Richardson, who was Chair of the Conference, is entirely justified. 'Children's religious education should have nothing to do with "nurturing" towards one faith. It should be purely educational and reflect the different faiths around them. Otherwise they will grow up ignorant and suspicious' *(Ealing and Southall Informer*, week ending 12th April). This kind of judgement made at the local level is well within the spirit and the letter of the government's interpretation of the Act.

If Ealing feels obliged to carry out a review and revision of its agreed syllabus, this need not be with respect to the balance of content but only to its particularity. The principle at stake here is quite fundamental for the future of religious education. The question is whether the subject is to offer equal opportunities and open access to all pupils, whether religious education is to be an educational activity available to all pupils regardless of their faith or lack of it, and whether it is to express in educational terms the legitimate spiritual aspirations of all sections of the community, or whether it is to be partisan, whether it will become impossible for pupils from the other principal religions to receive an appropriate religious education because what they study will be mainly Christian. Another equally unacceptable possibility is that pupils should be separated along religious lines, creating in England and Wales the divisions which have proved to be so destructive in Northern Ireland and in the Lebanon.

Problems in the DES interpretation

A number of difficulties are apparent in the legal advice passed on by the Secretary of State. For example, what is a 'principal religion represented in Great Britain'? Will we soon find that the Department of Education and Science will have to draw up a list of principal religions which must be included in any agreed syllabus similar to the lists of acceptable qualifications equivalent to a pass at GCSE mathematics? Such is the logic of an approach which seeks to define the content of religious education by law in terms like these. Does the Secretary of State look forward to the controversies which his Department will be engaged in with those religions which are excluded from his list?

Another problem relates to the tension between what most agreed syllabuses shall be like and the responsibility for balance which remains at the local level. If local authorities are to decide on the precise balance, and if that decision may go one way or the other, how can the government require that most of the syllabuses shall be balanced in one particular way? The answer appears to be that the Department of Education and Science assumes that decisions about the precise balance of content will reflect the religious composition of the local area. Where almost all the school population was Christian, active or passive, the local agreed syllabus might for that very reason insist that pupils gained a good understanding of a range of religions in order to offset the narrowness of the local environment. It is possible that the details provided for all the other principal religions might together slightly outweigh the Christianity content. Indeed, the Secretary of State's letter seems to suggest this when insisting that national as well as local factors should be borne in mind. An agreed syllabus must be relevant to its local community, but educational relevance is not a matter of reflecting in the syllabus the proportion of religions represented in the community. We are educating our pupils not for life around the village pump but for life in Great Britain, Europe and the world.

Is the legislation flawed?

Let us return to the question of the misleading publicity which surrounded the general letter of 18th March and the particular advice given to the London Boroughs. It is true that government has no particular control over the angle which the press will give to an item, but it seems regrettable that on such a delicate issue the Department of Education and Science did not see fit to issue a statement which would have directed the press toward the main character of the advice. Moreover, the government has done nothing to rectify the public misunderstanding which has arisen as a result of the one-sided treatment given in the press. Is this responsible government?

When it was learnt in the spring and summer of 1988 that the content of new agreed syllabuses was to be defined as set out in section 8(3) there was a general feeling that although not particularly desirable, the wording was acceptable. Informed teachers and tolerant parents did not welcome the wording, but it was accepted as something which could be lived with.

This acceptance was based on the belief that the wording could be interpreted in a manner so as to give equal opportunities and open access to all. If, as a result of the relentless pressure from some Christians and the persistent misunderstanding with which the press and media have conveyed it, it becomes impossible to defend the balance, it will become apparent that the legislation is flawed. The misgivings expressed in 1988, tempered by the belief that an educational interpretation was still possible, will flare up again. If a misunderstood law deprives the classrooms of equality and justice in religious education, and if it proves impossible to remove the misunderstanding, the next step can only be to remove the law. Those who insist upon an exaggerated Christian interpretation of the law are not its best friends.

Christianity in the Agreed Syllabuses

Autumn 1992

With its two thousand years of history and its twenty-five thousand denominations spread through every nation and language on earth, Christianity cannot fail to attract the attention of most branches of scholarship and research. It continues to be the focus for major philosophical questions, it is a living and growing inspiration for art and literature, it is profoundly intertwined with cultural questions including economic and political affairs, and it continues to engage in lively debate with almost every one of the natural and social sciences.

This poses a particular challenge to the teacher of religious education. Not only must he or she embrace as much as possible of the phenomenon of Christianity, including at least some aspects of its relationships with other disciplines, but it must be set within the framework of educational studies. This means that questions must be asked about what shall be taught and how. Moreover, these decisions must relate both to the lives of the pupils and to the cultural and institutional context within which the education takes place.

The problem of selection

In view of the size and complexity of Christianity, selection is inevitable. It is important therefore that selection should take place in accordance with informed and defensible principles. A number of such principles suggest themselves as possibilities.

1. Selection could reflect the interests and experience of the individual teacher. While it is easy to point out the dangers of this approach, it is more difficult to suggest realistic ways of overcoming them. If the teacher is of a religious or Christian outlook it can easily lead to a lack of critical perspective. The religious mind, immersed in what is taken for granted, may lack the flexibility which is necessary in any education process. Only through sustained programmes of professional training can the weaknesses of this first approach be overcome.

2. Selection may reflect the interests of pupils. While this perspective cannot be ignored, because there can be no effective teaching without it, the power of religious education to expand horizons will be diminished if the immediate interest of the pupil becomes the main criterion. Relevance to the interests of the pupil is actually a question of method rather than of content. The task is to *develop* the interests of the pupil, using them as a starting point.

3. Materials from Christianity could be selected using a framework developed from religious studies. The phenomenon of religion as a whole could be

categorized and Christian examples offered of each category. Thus if religion itself is to be divided up into various dimensions such as the historical, the doctrinal and the ethical, then aspects of Christianity which illustrate each of these could become the content.

4. The content of Christianity could be defined by Christians, by asking church authorities to define their faith. At first sight this seems an attractive possibility, but it presents difficulties. Statements of faith tend to be heavily doctrinal and are often rooted in a different historical context. Moreover, such summaries tend to be directed either towards teaching the faithful or justifying the existence of the denomination. The possibility that a church might present a summary of its life and teaching for some other purpose is an interesting challenge. In any case, who is to decide which denominations are invited to represent the Church as a whole by presenting their understanding of Christianity? It is not surprising that Christian education in the state schools of England and Wales has taken a different route.

5. Christianity could be taught by a 'single-discipline' approach – for example, a historical approach. To teach Christianity then becomes to teach Church history. An extension of this approach might use a different discipline for each key stage. Thus Key Stage 1 could be based on narrative Christianity, Key Stages 2 and 3 on historical Christianity, Key Stage 4 on philosophical and ethical Christianity. This approach is certainly worth exploring.

6. Another popular approach from the past may be described as the study of Christian origins. This is a version of the single-discipline approach through history, except that it confines the study of Christianity to the biblical period and justifies it not in the name of the historical discipline as such but in the name of some theory of classical essence. The Bible is studied not because it is historical but because it is the normative or classical expression of Christianity. This approach has much to commend it and needs reviving.

7. A further principle of selection would be the opposite of the previous one. One would concentrate on the modern world and contemporary issues. When Christianity is taught through contemporary theatre or film or when it is supported by such a discipline from the social sciences as ethnography, one has an attractive pattern of selection.

No doubt there are others, but these will do to illustrate the variety of problems in the selection of Christianity. No doubt, in their various ways, all of these and others should be developed and encouraged. The teaching of

Christianity will flourish in British schools in an atmosphere of creative curriculum development. It would be unwise to impose just one pattern of selection. That does not mean there cannot be progress towards a national curriculum of Christian religious education. Such a national curriculum should include curriculum alternatives and also alternative principles for creating curriculum alternatives.

The educational context

In the state schools of England and Wales the problem of Christian curriculum selection has been addressed since the mid-1920s through the machinery of the agreed syllabus. In effect, denominational selection of content was negotiated in an ecumenical climate with educational considerations occupying the foreground. Today we face a far more complex situation than the agreed syllabus was designed to deal with. Without a grasp of the factors involved it is impossible to understand why the problem of selection has become so urgent.

In the first place, denominational life within the Christian churches no longer offers the same kind of ideological enclosure as it used to. Almost everybody agrees that the real boundaries of Christian concern are no longer those between the traditional denominations. Secondly, the number of Christian denominations has greatly increased. Alongside those which are long-established, the needs and claims of other substantial Christian communities, often with an ethnic base, must be considered. Christianity is a world religion here in Britain, and we should not be unaware of the complexities of Christianity in mainland Europe.

Another factor in the break-up of the old conventions of selection is the emergence of religious studies as an academic discipline. The norms for the study of Christianity in the lecture theatre or the classroom are not the same as those for the pulpit or the Sunday school. Christian self-understanding, although an essential aspect of study, cannot have unchallenged supremacy in the public educational programmes of state schools in pluralist democracies. There is perhaps no area of the curriculum where the professional mediation of the teacher between the object of study and the pupil is more necessary than in the case of Christianity.

The nature of the Christian faith

While, as we have just seen, there are social and educational reasons why the problem of selecting a Christian curriculum has become more complex, the basic reasons for this complexity are not educational or administrative. They lie within the Christian faith itself. It is important to realize that the curriculum discussions about an appropriate method for the teaching of Christianity, whether it should be taught through themes and topics, whether it should be taught experientially or phenomenologically, whether it should be taught with other faiths or in isolation from them, are only superficially to be regarded as questions of religious education method. It is deeper than that. They are symptoms of different perspectives regarding the character of Christianity. The problem of curriculum selection in Christianity is not only educational; it is theological.

Four kinds of Christianity

There are several kinds of Christianity as well as several ways of communicating an understanding of the Christian faith. Perhaps further analysis may be added. First, there is a God Christianity. This is a Christianity centred upon universal, metaphysical principles, a Christianity which looks upon itself as a revelation of an eternal truth. Secondly, there is a Jesus Christianity, in which the believer and Jesus gaze upon each other. This is a Christianity of loving, personal devotion. Thirdly, there is an ego Christianity, a Christianity which serves the disguised interests of the self, the group or the nation. This is the national Christianity, the European Christianity, the white Christianity or the Christianity which serves the interests of the class consciousness which professes it. Finally, there is a Kingdom of God Christianity, a Christianity which stands side by side with Jesus rather than face to face. This is a Christianity which conceives of itself as discipleship, a Christianity which regards itself as the extension of the ministry and mission of Jesus.

Each of these Christianities has much to teach children and young people, to say nothing of adults. However, each is uneasy in the presence of the others. Which form of Christianity is most deeply imbued with the spirit of Jesus, with the Holy Spirit of God?

In his famous sermon on 'The Yoke of Religion' delivered more than forty years ago, Paul Tillich said:

It would not be worthwhile to teach Christianity, if it were for the sake of Christianity. And believe me, you who are estranged from Christianity, it is not our purpose to make you religious and Christian when we interpret the call of Jesus for our time. We call Jesus the Christ not because he brought a new religion, but because he is the end of religion, above religion and irreligion, above Christianity and non-Christianity. We spread his call because it is the call to every man in every period to receive the New Being....

The SCAA Model Syllabuses

Autumn 1994

*T*his passage was written, as the reference to Gillian Shephard as being the Secretary of State for Education indicates, at a time when the then government still had more than two years to run. A hope which was expressed at the end of the first section below proved to be futile. The Conservative administration had apparently decided that it had more than enough troubles without entering upon religious education controversies, and a good deal of the ideological fervour from the right wing disappeared. On 1st May 1997, a new Labour Government was elected. Schools can accept a readier recognition of religious diversity, and this may make it easier for religious educators to act upon the pluralistic requirements of the 1988 Education Reform Act. It is also possible that in the interests of equal opportunities and wider access, the less acceptable aspects of the legislation and, above all, of the departmental circular may be removed.

On 5th July 1994 some Model Syllabuses for Religious Education were published by the School Curriculum and Assessment Authority (SCAA). These are likely to fulfil an important function in asserting the plurality of religious education, since it is suggested that local agreed syllabuses should include courses on all of the major religions present in Great Britain, namely Christianity, Hinduism, Islam, Judaism, Sikhism and Buddhism. For several years there has been a rather fruitless controversy about the percentage of an agreed syllabus which should be devoted to the various religions. When the draft version of the SCAA model syllabuses was published for consultation on 25th January 1994, percentages had been dropped but there was still a chart indicating proportions of time to be devoted to the various religions. This made it clear that Christianity was to predominate and that other religions were to be reduced to a bare minimum. In the final form of the model syllabuses the chart has also been removed and we are thus left with a straightforward world religions syllabus which can be discussed on its own merits.

The new model syllabuses, or 'national guidelines' as they are sometimes rather misleadingly called, were immediately attacked by a number of Christian groups and individuals precisely because they did not establish an unambiguous position of dominance for Christianity. Leaders of all the religious communities, including the Christian churches and the Archbishop of Canterbury himself, responded by reaffirming the plurality of religious life in Britain, welcoming its variety and congratulating SCAA on its recognition of this fact. Relationships between major religious communities, having become a little uneasy owing to the competitive situation created by the insistence of some Christians upon a specified proportion of Christianity, seemed immediately to improve. Newspapers and television screens were suddenly flooded with warm, smiling faces of religious leaders welcoming each other and affirming their desire that children in school should learn from all the great faiths. The Department for Education, urged on by the Christian traditionalists, had been pressing for the predominance of Christianity, but it now went rather quiet and before the end of July a cabinet reshuffle had brought about a change in its leadership. Mr Patten and Baroness Blatch, neither of whom were noted for their recognition of the plurality of religious education, were replaced. It must now be hoped that under Gillian Shephard a more harmonious relationship between the Department and the profession will be created, based upon a new realism in recognizing the character of an appropriate religious education for modern young people.

Plurality is not enough

The publication of the model syllabuses has thus been a significant event in religious education, and those who worked so hard in producing them are to be congratulated on their efforts. They themselves will be amongst the first to recognize that further developments are necessary. The mere reassertion of plurality, important though it is in the present context, is not enough to guarantee a sound religious education. The problem is that the two syllabuses offered by SCAA are of the same type: each religion is presented separately. First there is a unit on Christianity, then one on Buddhism, one on Hinduism and so on. This type of syllabus is generally known as the 'systems approach', since religion is seen as divided into a number of separate religious systems, each one self-contained. There is certainly a place for this way of teaching religion, especially in the secondary school, but it has weaknesses as well as strengths, and it is a pity that no other type of syllabus is offered. When one remembers that separation between religions has been insisted upon by the Christian traditionalists, spurred on by their beliefs that the fundamental distinction in British society is between Christians and non-Christians, the approach must be regarded as ideologically suspect.

The law and the statutes

The truth is that the Christian traditionalists, supported so far by the government, have insisted upon a narrow interpretation of section 8(3) of the 1988 Education Reform Act. They have claimed that the famous clause which requires new agreed syllabuses to 'reflect the fact that the principal religious traditions in Great Britain are in the main Christian whilst taking account of the teaching and practices of the other principal religions represented in Great Britain' can only mean that the religious education syllabus should be taught in separate compartments, religion by religion. However, as long ago as 1980 the Department of Education had sought legal advice in order to enable the then Secretary of State to respond to a complaint referred to him in connection with the newly published agreed syllabuses in the London Boroughs of Ealing and Newham. This advice, dated 12th June 1990, states: 'The fact that the religious traditions in Great Britain are in the main Christian *could be* reflected by devoting most time to Christian traditions but in my opinion the *flexibility* inherent in the word 'reflect' means that this could be done in other ways, for example *by comparison with other religions* and discussion as to the differences and similarities between Christian and other traditions' (section 9(5), italics added).

It is astonishing that this advice was not relayed to the Chief Education Officers when the Department issued its circular letter of 18th March 1991. Clearly, the Christian traditionalists were embarrassed to find that the legislation is less clear-cut than they had supposed, and does not in fact endorse either a separation between religions or an unambiguous preponderance for Christianity. Accordingly, this piece of advice, so profoundly relevant and important to the religious education of the children of this country, was suppressed. Claims about the correct interpretation of the legislation became less strident after this advice was received, and other reasons were found for making the same points. By now the Department had realized that it did not have a leg to stand on if it was to continue to be led by the Christian traditionalists. This is the background to the publication of the model syllabuses on 5th July 1994. The end result is that the plural or world religions interpretation of the 1988 legislation is confirmed and has received general approval.

A problem remains, however, in that the model syllabuses are still based upon the assumption of separation and not upon the assumption of mutuality and dialogue. The SCAA model syllabuses do not provide for a study of the religious dimension of human experience, nor do they conceive of human beings as confronting certain questions of meaning and purpose which find responses in the actual religions of the world. The generic study of religion disappears entirely. There is no recognition of the fact that the religious history of humanity is indivisible, that no religion has evolved in isolation from other religions, or that the interest of young people is engaged when they see religions addressing living issues. It is because of these significant omissions that the model syllabuses must be supplemented by others.

Postscript

Perhaps there is a deep-rooted clash of values between education as a drawing out and a maturing of the human, and the character of the modern state, which has emerged since the late Middle Ages as a centre of power, consolidated around its territory and its currency, in competition with other similar organizations of money and land. Perhaps these opposing values will be reconciled as the unification of Europe continues in the years to come, but that will depend upon the emerging relationship between the European Community and the rest of the world. However, until the day comes when human lives are no longer determined by the accumulation of power through control over money and territory, until the day when 'the wolf shall live with the lamb, the leopard shall lie down with the kid, the calf and the lion and the fatling together, and a little child shall lead them' (Isaiah 11:6), there will continue to be a conflict of values. The values of democracy, of a commonwealth in which the resources of the land are equally available to all of its people, will continue to be in conflict with the values of the money-god, the values determined first and foremost by the desire to accumulate money. Since the religions are the major disciplines for the transformation of the human spirit, and since the task of religious education is to enable children and young people to come into contact with religion, a contact which will be both critical and spiritual, it is likely that religious education will continue to stand in the centre of this conflict of values.

The religions of the world may be described as the utopian projects of the human spirit. For all of their ancient patriarchal origins, the rigidity which they so easily produce, and the competitive relationships between them which have so often turned them against each other, religion remains the most potent expression of longing for a world society based upon transformed brotherhood and sisterhood. This does not mean that religion is necessary, in the strict sense, in order to bring about this human transformation. The aim of religious education in school is certainly not to make boys and girls more religious. However, the religions undoubtedly represent a resource for human development. They dramatize the adventures of the human spirit, in both darkness and light, in both glory and tragedy. The imagination of young people needs to be challenged through encounter with these traditions.

This is why religious education in our schools will continue to be a utopian project. Without such whispers of utopia, the imagination of our young people is likely to be limited to the conceptions of life conveyed so powerfully night and day by the values of our money-mad world.

Further Reading

This book records the development from the early 1970s through to 1995 of the rationale for religious education as practised in Britain. Of course, this has been surrounded by controversy, and the rationale presented in this book is not the only one. However, it can be said to represent a mainstream, and the reading list which follows is offered as a guide to those who want to pursue the rationale itself and some of its applications in practice.

Probably the most substantial and sustained exploration of this rationale for religious education is to be found in Michael H. Grimmitt's *Religious Education and Human Development: the relationship between studying religions and personal, social and moral education* (McCrimmon, 1987), while the most successful attempt to found the subject within one of the social sciences is Robert Jackson's *Religious Education: an interpretive approach* (London, Hodder & Stoughton, 1997). A good collection of periodical articles is provided by Jeff Astley and Leslie J. Francis (eds), *Christian Theology and Religious Education: connections and contradictions* (London, SPCK, 1996).

Amongst books from an earlier period, reference may be made to J. W. D. Smith's *Religions and secular education* (Edinburgh, St Andrew Press, 1975) and Edwin Cox, *Problems and possibilities for religious education* (London, Hodder & Stoughton, 1983).

As illustrations of the research base, one should consult Leslie J. Francis, William K. Kay and William S. Campbell (eds), *Research in religious education* (Leominster, Gracewing, 1996) and Kenneth E. Hyde, *Religion in childhood and adolescence: a comprehensive review of the research* (Birmingham, Alabama, REP, 1990), which has become a standard reference work. The Westhill Project, edited by Garth Read, John Rudge, Geoff Teece and Roger B. Howarth, *How do I teach RE?* (Cheltenham, Stanley Thornes, second edition 1992) provides a guide to both curriculum theory and practice, and Dennis Starkings (ed.), *Religion and the Arts in Education: dimensions of spirituality* (Sevenoaks, Hodder & Stoughton Educational, 1993) offers a number of studies relating the subject to creativity.

Turning to the secondary school, Michael Kincade, *How to improve learning in RE* (London, Hodder & Stoughton, 1991) is recommended, and of the many good practical guides to religious education in the primary school, I have found the following to be particularly useful: Robert Jackson and Dennis Starkings, *The Junior RE Handbook* (Cheltenham, Stanley Thornes, 1990), Derek Bastide (ed.), *Good practice in primary religious education, 4–11* (London, Falmer, 1992) and Geoff Teece, *How to write your scheme of work for RE: religious education in the primary school* (Birmingham, Westhill College, 1996).

There are two excellent books recently published on collective worship in school: Derek Webster's *Collective worship in schools: contemporary approaches* (Cleethorpes, Kenelm Press, 1995) and Elaine McCreery's *Worship in the primary school* (London, Fulton, 1993).

Finally, Terence Copley, *Teaching Religion: fifty years of religious education in England and Wales* (Exeter, University of Exeter Press, 1997) offers a lively and readable account of the history of the subject, placing it within the context of contemporary social and political life.

Chronological List of Journal Articles

Index